Frederic William Farrar

Ephphatha or the Amelioration of the World

sermons preached at West minister Abbey

Frederic William Farrar

Ephphatha or the Amelioration of the World
sermons preached at West minister Abbey

ISBN/EAN: 9783744715041

Printed in Europe, USA, Canada, Australia, Japan

Cover: Foto ©Lupo / pixelio.de

More available books at **www.hansebooks.com**

EPHPHATHA

OR

The Amelioration of the World

SERMONS PREACHED AT WESTMINSTER ABBEY
WITH TWO SERMONS
PREACHED IN ST. MARGARET'S CHURCH
AT
THE OPENING OF PARLIAMENT

BY

F. W. FARRAR, D.D., F.R.S.

CANON OF WESTMINSTER, AND RECTOR OF ST. MARGARET'S, WESTMINSTER

London
MACMILLAN AND CO.
AND NEW YORK
1892

The Right of Translation and Reproduction is Reserved

TO THE VERY REV.

ARTHUR PENRHYN STANLEY, D.D.,

DEAN OF WESTMINSTER,

THAN WHOM FEW LIVING MEN HAVE SHOWN

A DEEPER INTEREST IN EVERY GOOD WORK WHICH CAN

HELP FORWARD THE HAPPINESS OF ALL CLASSES,

WHETHER RICH OR POOR,

These Sermons are Dedicated

WITH SINCERE AFFECTION AND RESPECT.

PREFACE.

THE seven Sermons which give their title to this little volume were preached in the ordinary course of my duties at Westminster Abbey during the months of December 1879 and January 1880. I publish them partly in obedience to the requests of many who desired to possess them in a permanent form, but chiefly because they carry out one consecutive line of thought, and deal with some topics which are not frequently touched upon in pulpit exhortations.

"Pauperism," it has been said, is national dishonour; so is drunkenness; so is preventible disease; so is the miserable squalor in which our poorest classes in the large towns live, even when they escape the workhouse.

These are the most real and formidable enemies we have (as a nation) to contend with, and if we attack them sincerely, we shall have fighting enough to last our time.[1] If these Sermons be even in a very slight degree effectual in diverting the thoughts of Christians from controversies about things doubtful or non-essential,—if they tend to deepen the feeling of mutual charity among all who earnestly desire to carry on the work of Christ in the world,—they will have fulfilled the object which has mainly induced me to let them see the light. If the main thoughts here urged be true and right, perhaps others may pursue them with greater power and more advantage to the general good.

We are told by Bishop Burnett that it was the noble study of the Cambridge Platonists " to propagate better thoughts, to take men off from being in parties, or from narrow notions, superstitious conceits, and fierceness

[1] Speech of Lord Derby at the Mansion House, March 1st, 1880.

about opinions." They endeavoured to achieve these aims by their large catholicity of spirit in dealing with questions of theology; but the same end may perhaps be also furthered by the humble endeavour to call attention to those vast fields of labour in which all sects and classes of Christians may strenuously and joyfully take a common part.

The eighth and ninth Sermons were preached at my own church at the opening of two sessions of Parliament. They may perhaps serve to show that it is possible for a clergyman without offence to deal with questions which may be fairly called political. They were kindly received by many members of Parliament who differ in their political views, and their publication was even requested by some of these, as well as by one whose high rank and office might well entitle him to regard his request almost in the light of a command.

The last Sermon was preached in the Abbey in June 1879. This Sermon also touches more or less on political considerations, and is added to the rest in obedience to a wish which I could not disregard.

Perhaps it is superfluous to say even thus much about these few Sermons. Apart from the living voice, and such interest as may have been derived from the places and circumstances in which they were spoken, they can but be regarded as dead leaves. Yet even dead leaves may have their use. "They will reach the hands of the reader chill and discoloured; but when, in the autumn evenings, the leaves fall and lie on the ground, more than one glance may still fall on them, more than one hand still gather them. And even if they were despised of all alike, the wind may sweep them away, and prepare with them a couch for some poor man, on whom Providence looks down with love from the height of heaven."

F. W. FARRAR.

St. Margaret's Rectory, Westminster

CONTENTS.

SERMON I.
WHY JESUS SIGHED . . . . PAGE 1

SERMON II.
SINCERITY OF HEART AS THE FIRST CONDITION OF SERVICE 41

SERMON III.
ENERGY OF CHRISTIAN SERVICE 79

SERMON IV.
THE WINGS OF A DOVE 119

SERMON V.
WORK IN THE GROANING CREATION 153

SERMON VI.
THE MENDING AND MARRING OF HUMAN LIFE . . 191

SERMON VII.

LAST LESSONS FROM THE SIGH OF CHRIST 225

SERMON VIII.

LEGISLATIVE DUTIES 259

SERMON IX.

THE AIMS OF CHRISTIAN STATESMANSHIP 287

SERMON X.

MANY FOLDS: ONE FLOCK 315

SERMON I.

WHY JESUS SIGHED:

THE SIGH OF PITY A STIMULUS TO ACTION.

WHY JESUS SIGHED.

Almighty God, who hast given thine only Son to be unto us both a sacrifice for sin, and also an ensample of godly life; give us grace that we may always most thankfully receive that His inestimable benefit, and also daily endeavour ourselves to follow the blessed steps of His most holy life, through the same Jesus Christ our Lord. Amen.

"Pereant commenta philosophorum qui negant in sapientem cadere perturbationes animorum."—AUG. *in Joann.* xiii. 21.

"Sight so deform what heart of rock could long
  Dry-eyed behold? Adam could not, but wept,
Though not of woman born: compassion quell'd
His best of man, and gave him up to tears
A space, till firmer thoughts restrained excess,
And scarce recovering words, his plaint renew'd :—
  'O miserable Mankind, to what fall·
Degraded, to what wretched state reserv'd!'"
        MILTON, *Paradise Lost*, xi. 494—510.

"Ahi quanto a dir quel era è cosa dura
  Questa selva selvaggia ed aspra e forte,
  Che nel pensier rinnova la paura !
Tanto è amara, che poco è piu morte."
        DANTE, *Inferno*, 1. 4—7.

SERMON I.

WHY JESUS SIGHED.

MARK VII. 34.

"*And looking up to heaven, He sighed, and saith unto him, Ephphatha! that is, 'Be opened.'*" [1]

THE incident to which this verse alludes happened during that period of wandering—we might almost say of flight—in foreign and half-heathen countries, which was forced upon our

[1] Καὶ ἀναβλέψας εἰς τὸν οὐρανὸν, ἐστέναξε, καὶ λέγει αὐτῷ, Ἐφφαθά, ὅ ἐστι, Διανοίχθητι.

In the English version of the text we may notice (α) that a more definite sense would be given to the word διανοίχθητι by rendering it "Be *thou* opened." The miraculous command seems to be addressed to the sufferer himself, whose whole existence is, as it were, closed by his being deaf and dumb. Further, the aorist implies that the result was instantaneous; and the compound verb that it was complete.

(β) The heavenward glance was doubtless a glance of prayer

Lord by the hatred and jealousy of the religious authorities of His nation, after the brief year

(John xi. 41), and served incidentally to refute those who attributed the Lord's miracles to evil powers (Matt. ix. 34; Mark iii. 22; Luke xi. 15), which was a favourite slander of the Pharisees.

(γ) The word ἐστέναξε might equally well be rendered "He groaned," as the same verb is rendered in Rom. viii. 23, "even we ourselves groan within ourselves"; 2 Cor. v. 2, "for in this we groan," and verse 4. In Heb. xiii. 17, μὴ στενάζοντες is rendered "not with grief;" and in James v. 9, μὴ στενάζετε κατ' ἀλλήλων is rendered "grudge not one against another," with the marginal alternative of "groan" or "grieve not." There is no more exact word in Greek, as there is in Latin, to differentiate a sigh from a groan. In the LXX. στενάζω is used as the rendering for various Hebrew verbs implying outward expressions of sadness.

In the English Version "sighing" and "groaning" are alike used as renderings of the Hebrew *ânach, anâchâh* (*e.g.* Job iii. 24, "my sighing;" *id.* xxiii. 2, "my groaning;" Ps. vii. 6, "I am weary with my groaning;" Ps. xxxi. 10, "my years with sighing," &c.). The substantive στεναγμός is rendered "groaning" in Acts vii. 34, Rom. viii. 26. The words rendered " He groaned in the spirit," and " Jesus therefore again groaning in Himself," in John xi. 33, 38, are different. See n. 3, p. 8.

(δ) The word *Ephphatha* is variously regarded as a Greek transliteration of the Aramaic imperative Hithpahel of *Pâthach*, "he opened," or as the imperative Niphal of that verb. (Comp. Is. xxxv. 5, "then shall the ears of the deaf be unstopped.")

(ε) It may be asked why the Evangelist, writing for Roman readers, reproduces the Aramaic word, which they would not understand, as he does also in v. 41, *Talitha Cumi;* x. 51, of His acceptable ministry on the shores of Lake Gennesareth.¹ He was returning to Galilee, apparently by devious paths, and on the lonelier eastern side of the lake, when they brought to Him a poor deaf stammerer, and besought Him to put His hand upon him. Never indifferent to the appeal of sorrow, Jesus led the poor man aside, put His fingers into his ears, spat, and touched his tongue, and then raising His eyes to Heaven for one brief moment of silent prayer to His

---

Rabboni (in the Greek); xv. 34, *Eloi, Eloi, lama sabachthani*. The answer is, that these are introduced because they had made on St. Peter—who, according to early tradition, furnished these narratives to St. Mark—an impression so indelible that no other words seemed adequate to give it force. Incidentally they are valuable as bearing on the question of the language which our Lord ordinarily spoke.

It is for a somewhat different reason that St. Mark and the other Evangelists so freely availed themselves of many other technical terms (Pharisees, Sadducees, Rabbi, Corban, Abba, Boanerges, Gehenna, &c.). They used them because no one equivalent word, and even no periphrasis, would have adequately conveyed their exact meaning, and it was better to give currency to an unfamiliar term than to employ an inadequate and misleading translation of it.

¹ Perhaps I may be allowed to refer, by way of elucidation of these expressions, to my *Life of Christ*, i. 473 to ii. 40.

Heavenly Father, *He sighed* and said unto him, "*Ephphatha!*" that is, "*Be opened!*"

1. This is not the only record of the sighs, and tears, and troubled heart of Jesus. We are told in the Epistle to the Hebrews, that "in the days of His flesh He offered up supplications, with strong crying and tears."[1] We read in the next chapter of St. Mark, how, when He was met by the Pharisees with the faithless and mocking demand for a sign from heaven, He sighed deeply in His spirit.[2] And by the grave of Lazarus, when He saw Mary weeping, and the Jews also weeping, He "groaned in the spirit," and the silent tears streamed down His face.[3] And on that day

---

[1] Heb. v. 7, μετὰ κραυγῆς ἰσχυρᾶς καὶ δακρύων.

[2] Mark viii. 12, ἀναστενάξας τῷ πνεύματι αὐτοῦ.

[3] John xi. 33, ἐνεβριμήσατο τῷ πνεύματι. 38, ἐμβριμώμενος ἐν ἑαυτῷ. The expressions which I have used are sufficiently supported by verse 35 (ἐδάκρυσεν ὁ Ἰησοῦς, which means that He shed silent tears), but the verb in verses 33 and 38 can hardly mean "groaned." In the New Testament it only occurs elsewhere in Matt. ix. 30, Mark i. 43, where it is rendered "straitly charged," though it is in reality more emphatic. A comparison of these verses with Luke v. 14, seems to show that the meaning involved in the verb is "vehemently threatened"; comp. Ecclus. xiii. 3. In the Old Testament the verb is used by Symmachus in Is. xvii. 13 (E.V. "rebuke"),

of humble triumph when the multitude escorted Him from Bethany to Jerusalem with shouted Hosannas and waving palms, as soon as He turned the shoulder of the hill, and the view of

and the noun by the LXX. in Lam. ii. 6; and wherever it occurs it always seems to imply indignation rather than grief. If τῷ πνεύματι is the dative of the object, the phrase can only express an act of strong self-control ("He sternly charged His spirit"—roused His spirit to the conflict with Death). If, on the other hand, τῷ πνεύματι means "in spirit," as in xiii. 21, then the expression means "He was indignant in spirit"; indignant at the want of faith of those around Him, or at the powerful presentment of the sin and sorrow of the world which was forced upon His notice by the circumstances of the moment. Some have supposed that the remark of the Jews in John xi. 37 was a sort of mocking taunt. This would indeed account for His feeling of indignation; but the Jews seem to have felt a genuine sympathy with the weeping sisters, and the remark—which was only made by *some* of them—has an accent of sincerity.

The words translated "and was troubled" are literally "and troubled Himself." This certainly does not mean that He only allowed Himself a certain definite amount of emotion (μετριοπάθεια as opposed to the Stoic apathy). This sense is attached by St. Cyril, Euthymius, and Theophylact to the previous expression (ἐνεβριμήσατο τῷ πνεύματι), and Theophylact comments on it by saying that hard and unsympathetic tearlessness is monstrous (θηριῶδες), but that *undue* indulgence in tears and lamentations is effeminate (γυναικῶδες). They are followed by Bengel, who says that, at this point, Jesus sternly checked the tears which, a little later He allowed to flow. In the *Life of Christ*, ii. 169, I rejected the city burst on Him, He wept aloud[1] over its hypocrisy and crime. Truly he was "a man of sorrows and acquainted with grief." So, to some extent, have all His saints and children been. "Prosperity," as has been justly said, "is consistent with intense worldliness, intense selfishness, intense hardness of heart, while the grander features of human character, self-sacrifice, disregard of pleasure, patriotism, knowledge, devotion to any great cause, have no tendency to bring good fortune. The wrongs, the cruelties, the wretchedness of all kinds which

the analogous explanation of "He troubled Himself," for that of Euthymius and Meyer, who explain it of a physical act—"a powerful shudder ran through Him" (as a consequence, Euthymius adds, of the stern repression of His feelings). On careful reconsideration of the passage I incline to the view that it implies the voluntary act by which our Lord suffered His sympathy to have play; yielded Himself to the deep emotions of the hour, and suffered those emotions to express themselves by outward signs. [In other passages we find the more ordinary passive xiii. 21, ἐταράχθη τῷ πνεύματι; xii. 27, νῦν ἡ ψυχή μου τετάρακται.]

Thus the two phrases together imply a mixture of indignation and grief; the indignation stirred by close contact with the workings of sin and death; the grief awakened by the sight of overwhelming sorrow.

[1] Luke xix. 14, ἔκλαυσεν, *ploravit*; ἐδάκρυσεν, *flevit*.

for ever prevail among mankind, his own shortcomings, of which he grows ever more and more conscious, these things will prevent a noble-minded man from ever being particularly light-hearted; so that if you see a man happy as the world goes, contented with himself, and contented with what is around him, he may be decent and respectable, but the highest is not in him, and the highest will not come out of him."[1] But in the case of Jesus, you must add the mysterious agony of Him who bore the vast burden, not of individual sins, but of the sins and sorrows of all mankind.[2] You must not indeed suppose that our blessed Saviour had no bright and joyous hours on earth, or that the legend is true which says that men had seen Him weep often, but never smile.[3] I believe that in those long quiet earlier years which "breathed beneath the Syrian blue" in Nazareth,—as a child, as a boy, as a youth, among its happy

---

[1] Froude, *Short Studies*, i. p. 111.
[2] Matt. viii. 17; Is. liii. 4; 1 Pet. ii. 24.
[3] Letter of the pseudo-Lentulus, Hofmann, *Leben Jesu*, p. 291; B. H. Cowper, *Apoc. Gospels*, p. 221.

children, and on its fresh thyme-sprinkled hills
—He drank sweet draughts of joy and sunlight.
I believe that in His words of gentle and almost
playful irony to Martha, and to Philip, and to
Peter,[1] we may almost see the heavenly smile
playing upon His features; and once we are
expressly told not only that He "was glad," but
that He "*exulted*" in spirit, as He also bade His
disciples do.[2] This joy of Jesus,—deep joy,
though noble and subdued—is not our subject
to-day, but I touch on it for one moment only
lest any of you should take a false view of the
life of man, or fatally imagine that in this world
the children of the devil have a monopoly of
happiness. Happiness?—they have none. *Guilty*
happiness? there is no such thing![3] Guilty
pleasure for a moment there is;—the sweetness

---

[1] See Luke x. 40; John xiv. 9; Matt. xvii. 26, and Luther's remarks on the latter passage.

[2] Luke x. 21, ἠγαλλιάσατο τῷ πνεύματι. Matt. v. 12, χαίρετε καὶ ἀγαλλιᾶσθε. For other instances in which the word occurs see Luke i. 47; John v. 35, viii. 56; Acts ii. 26.

[3] "Crede mihi res severa est verum gaudium."—*Sen. Ep.* xxiii. 92. "Cette joie dont je parle est sévère, chaste, sérieuse, solitaire, et incompatible."—BOSSUET, *Serm. sur la Circoncision.*

of the cup whose draught is poison, the glitter of the serpent whose bite is death. Guilty *mirth* there is;—the laughter of fools, which is as the crackling of thorns under a pot. But guilty happiness there never has been in any life, nor ever can there be. True happiness, happiness in the midst of even scorn and persecution, happiness even in the felon's prison and in the martyr's flame, is the high prerogative of God's saints alone—of God's saints, and therefore assuredly, even in His earthly life, of Him the King of Saints; since there is in misery but *one* intolerable sting, the sting of iniquity, and He had none.

2. But you will not have failed to notice that on two of the occasions on which we are told that Jesus sighed and wept, He was immediately about to dispel the cause of the misery.[1] He was about to heal the deaf. Why then should He have sighed? He was about to raise the dead. Why then did the silent tears stream down His face?

[1] Mark vii. 34; John xi. 36.

My friends, the Lord sighed because He was not thinking only of the individual case. *That* He had power to remedy; but how many myriads were there of the bereaved whom He could not then console? of the deaf and dumb who in this world could never hear and never speak? Even in the individual cases there was, to His quick sympathy, cause enough to sigh for the wreck caused by the sin of man and the malice of Satan, in deforming the beauty of God's fair creation. His sigh for these was not the sigh of Powerlessness—it was the sigh of Sympathy.[1] But more than this, He was thinking of all the world, looking down to the very depths of its drear abyss of sorrow. His act of healing could be but a drop in the ocean. "That sigh," says Luther, "was not drawn from Him on

---

[1] At the same time we should bear in mind that the sympathy of our Lord, even as sympathy, was something more intense, something more deep and mysterious, than the ordinary sympathy of which we are capable. In some unspeakable manner He bore, as though it were His own, the burden of our griefs and iniquities. Is. liii. 4; Matt. viii. 17 (ἔλαβε ... ἐβάστασε); John i. 29 (αἴρων); 1 Pet. ii. 24 (αὐτὸς ἀνήνεγκεν ... ἐπὶ τὸ ξύλον).

account of the single tongue and ears of this poor man, but it is a common sigh over all tongues and ears, yea over all hearts, bodies, and souls, and over all men, from Adam to his last descendant."[1] The doing of good is not a work of unmixed happiness, for good men can never do all the good that they desire. "We can, indeed, only have the highest happiness, such as goes along with being a great man, by having wide thoughts and much feeling for the rest of the world as well as for ourselves; and this sort of happiness often brings so much pain with it, that we can only tell it from pain by its being what we should choose before everything."[2] What wonder then that our Saviour, even in the act of healing, heaved the deep sigh of sympathy?

---

[1] So too St. Chrysostom, who says that Jesus sighed, τὴν τοῦ ἀνθρώπου φύσιν ἐλεῶν εἰς ποίαν ταπείνωσιν ἤγαγεν ταύτην ὅ τε μισόκαλος διάβολος καὶ ἡ τῶν πρωτοπλάστων ἀπροσεξία,—*i.e.* because He pitied the humiliation to which our human nature has been reduced by the Devil, who hates all fairness, and by the incontinence of our first parents.

[2] *Romola.*

> "O'erwhelming thoughts of pain and grief
>   Over his sinking spirit sweep;
> What boots it gathering one lost leaf
>   Out of yon sere and withered heap,
> Where souls and bodies, hopes and joys,
> All that earth owns, or sin destroys,
> Under the spurning hoof are cast
> Or tossing in the autumnal blast?"[1]

3. My friends, there was in truth cause enough, and more than enough, why the Lord should sigh. In that poor afflicted man He saw but one more sign of that vast crack and flaw which sin causes in everything which God has made. When God had finished His work, He saw that it was very good; but since then tares have been sown amid His harvest; an alien element intruded into His world; a jangling discord clashed into His music. Earth is no longer Eden. Look out even on the inanimate creation; its storm, and earthquake, and eclipse; the devastating fury of its elements; the pitiless rush of its waters; the deadly pestilence of its malaria; the invisible germs of corruption which impregnate its waters with pollution and people

[1] Keble, "Twelfth Sunday after Trinity."

its air with death:—these surely are signs of something wrong somewhere. Or look at the animal world, and the finish and frightfulness of the lethal armour with which it is provided,— the shark's teeth, the hornet's sting, the tiger's claw, the serpent's fang. What do we see? Not the lion lying down with the lamb, or the leopard playing with the kid; but the bright creatures bounding through the forest with hungry rage, and the dull eye of the snake in the dry leaves. Nay, there is massacre daily going on, daily raging among the blithe birds of the air, and the mute fishes of the sea. The air, the field, the wave are one vast slaughter house.[1] What is the meaning of it all, but this,— that the whole creation groaneth and travaileth in pain together until now?[2] And was there not

---

[1] "The May-fly is torn by the swallow, the swallow speared by the shrike,
And the whole little wood where I sit is a world of plunder and prey."—TENNYSON.

[2] Rom. viii. 22—25, where the words of the original—συστενάζει καὶ συνωδίνει ἄχρι τοῦ νῦν—are very powerful. But

enough in this rapine and fury to make Jesus look up to Heaven and sigh?

4. And alas, it is not only the unintelligent creation which groans and travails. We ourselves, which have the firstfruits of the Spirit, we ourselves also groan within ourselves, waiting for the adoption, to wit the redemption of the body. We are apt to be very proud of ourselves and of our marvellous discoveries and scientific achievements; but, after all, what a feeble creature is man! what a little breed his race! what shadows we are, and what shadows we pursue! We fade as the grass, and are crushed before the moth. If we knew no more than Nature can tell us, and had no help but what Science can give to us, what sigh would be too deep for beings born to sorrow as the sparks fly upwards? "Man that is born of a woman hath but a short time to live, and is full of misery;" so we say at the solemn truthful moment when we drop the body

---

the universal groan is full of hopefulness, for it is represented as being called forth by the travail-pangs of a new birth.

into the grave, and man is full of misery indeed!

i. Look, for instance, at the world of disease and pain. You need not go far to look. One house will suffice you to see the wretchedness of the human race.[1] We are met in this great Abbey close beside the Palaces of the Legislature, and on one side of us is Westminster Hospital, and on the other St. Thomas's Hospital, as though to bear their solemn witness how vast is the task before us, how dread is the necessity for religion and for government, to battle against human sin and human pain. Go into either of these great hospitals, and what will you see? Oh, what varied evidences of human anguish! On that bed lies a strong workman, crippled for life by an accident, and forgetting his own pain as the tears rush into his eyes to think of his worn wife and starving little ones. That little child, trained on gin,

[1] " Humani generis mores tibi nosse volenti,
Sufficit una domus; paucos consume dies et
Dicere te miserum, postquam illinc veneris aude."
—Juv. *Sat.* xiii. 159.

and screaming for every bottle which it thinks must contain gin, is dying of atrophy, the result of vile neglect. That poor half-witted old woman ends here, in the anguish of some inward complaint, her harmless life of unbroken struggle with affliction. The muttering lips, the clutching hands of yonder man are the signs of the fell disease which is the Nemesis of drunkenness. The bones of that other, the victim of dissolute courses, are full of the sin of his youth, which shall lie down with him in the dust. And Jesus had seen such things. He had healed the impotent man at Bethesda, and the frenzied boy at Hermon, and the poor wretch who was deaf and dumb, and blind and mad at Capernaum; and the ten lepers at En Gaunim; and had seen—

> "All maladies
> Of ghastly spasm, or racking torture, qualms
> Of heart-sick agony, all feverous kinds,
> Convulsions, epilepsies, fierce catarrhs;"[1]

and many more which I dare not dwell upon,

---

[1] Milton, *Par. Lost*, xi. 480.

—and can you wonder that He looked up to heaven and sighed?

ii. We have been glancing at some of the conditions which affect the physical world of man; the anguish which, in one form or another, by sickness or by accident, seizes ere we die the poor mortal bodies of most of us; but ah! that is not the worst. In the terrible picture of the "Last Judgment," by Michael Angelo, in the Sistine Chapel at Rome,—where the great painter's conception of Him who sighed for human sorrow, is an awful avenging figure, with hand wrathfully uplifted, grasping ten thousand thunders, and hurling down men's souls by millions into the abyss,—he has painted one lost spirit who is being dragged down by a horrible fiend. This fiend has driven his fangs into the flesh of the doomed victim; but the poor wretch is wholly unconscious of the agony; he is looking up in *mental* anguish, thinking only of the lost heaven. Even so it is that the sorrows of the body are swallowed up in the keener anguish of the soul, and the wounded affection aches more painfully than the throbbing nerve. Look, then, at the world of man's heart. How sweet is the unbroken home; how happy! Ah, but of what brittle glass is this our home-happiness made! How many of our homes *are* unbroken? into how many has the silent shadow never glided? how many have not been overshadowed by the icy hand? Ye who have reached middle age, has not your path in life been marked by the gravestones of your earlier friends? Has the light of your eyes been taken from none of you at a stroke? Fathers, have none of you followed to the tomb the dear youth who should have been the prop of your old age? Mothers, have you never seen the dust strewn on the little flower-like face? Will there be no vacant chairs this Christmas by your firesides? Weep not; we shall go to them, though they shall not return to us. "Oh Ibrahim, Ibrahim," exclaimed Mahomet—over the body of his dead child—"if it were not that the promise is faithful, and the hope of resurrection sure; if it were not that this is the way to be trodden by all, and the last of us shall join the first; I would grieve for thee with a grief deeper even than this," and with uncontrollable sobbings the strong man put the little body back into the nurse's arms. "I am torn up by the roots and lie prostrate on the earth," wrote Edmund Burke on the loss of his only son. "I am now old, feeble, bent, and miserable," said Sir William Napier, "and my eyes are dim, very dim, with weeping for my lost child." —How many millions of the nameless have had to utter the same bitter wail!

But this has been going on for ever, and Jesus had seen it all. He had seen, laid stark upon the bier, the widow's only son. He had seen the little maid of Jairus lying pale and cold. He had seen Mary weeping for Lazarus dead. And, as He looked out upon a world of death, can you wonder, I ask again, if, *looking up to heaven, He sighed?*

iii. For even this, alas, was not all, and not the worst. Sickness may be cured; and pain assuaged; and Time lays his healing hand on the wounds of death. And again sickness may be as the fire purging the gold; and when we think of the death of the righteous, we hardly dare to wish them back again. In all these things there may be a soul of goodness in things evil. But oh, the ravages of sin! there is mischief, and unmingled mischief, there. It is told of Queen Blanche of Navarre, mother of St. Louis of France, that she often said she would rather see her son a corpse at her feet, than know that he had committed a deadly sin. It is told of another sad queen, Queen Marie Antoinette of France, that to her the sorrow which, like Aaron's rod, swallowed up all other sorrows, was to know what vile hands would have the training of her princely boy.[1] But is that sorrow of

---

[1] "This fear it was—a fear like this I have often thought—which must among her other woes have been the Aaron-woe that swallowed up all the rest to the unhappy Marie Antoinette. This must have been the sting of death to her maternal heart, the grief paramount, the crowning grief,—the thought, namely, that her royal boy would not be dismissed from the honours of royalty to peace and humble innocence; but that his fair cheek would be ravaged by vice as well as by sorrow; that he would

watching the degeneracy of a bright life, the corruption of an innocent spirit,—is it a strange, abnormal sorrow? Has no parent among you had to send a child to start for life in some great school, or in some great city, and watched with an aching heart "the fine gradations of vice or intemperance by which the clear-browed boy has grown into the sullen, troubled, dissatisfied youth"? Would the story of the Prodigal have touched as it *has* touched the heart of the world if it were rare? Does the world offer at this moment an exhilarating spectacle? Wars costing so many precious lives; sedition trying to rear its head; reckless, murderous conspiracies; widespread distress; the sinfulness of waste; the baseness of dishonesty; the adulteration of food; selfish luxury; mad greed of gain; houses where, because of bad passions, the fires of hell mix with the hearth; the

be tempted into brutal orgies and every mode of moral pollution, until, like poor Constance with her young Arthur, but for a sadder reason, even if it were possible that the royal mother should see her son in the courts of heaven, she would not know again one so fearfully transfigured."—DE QUINCEY, *Autobiog. Sketches.*

reeling army of drunkards; the miserable victims of man's most degraded selfishness doomed by thousands to loathly lives and loathlier deaths; rancours in the political world, rancours yet more deadly in the so-called religious world; slander, and lies, and libels never more infamously rampant; the hearts of good men made sad which God hath not made sad; men hateful and hating one another;—is it altogether a glad spectacle, a happy spectacle? And all this too had Jesus seen. He had seen the petty tyranny of the Herods. He had seen angry and unscrupulous religionists—hating each other for differences of opinion, dealing in plausible disparagements and base insinuations, scheming and plotting to veil deadly hatreds under decent forms. He had seen Pharisees raging at Sadducees, and Sadducees sneering at Pharisees, and both alike conspiring, in the interests of a sham religion, to murder Him; and He had seen the riot of the prodigal, and the anguish of the adulteress; and the shame of the publican had moved his compassion; and the tears of the penitent harlot had fallen on His feet.—And once more, I ask, can you wonder if, as Jesus thus looked on the world of Sickness, the world of Death, the world of Sin, He looked up to Heaven, and sighed?

5. But why, my brethren, have I thus set before you this sad picture as it is? Not, be assured, with no object, although I think that the mere recognition of such facts is most needful sometimes for our callous selfishness and fastidious sensibility. It is good, it is right, to startle, if possible, the hard indifference of that vulgar English comfort and domesticity, which does nothing, and gives so shamefully little, for the sorrow around it. And the reason why it is right and useful is because there is a remedy for many of those evils; and the sigh for all the misery around us is but the passing expression of a sympathy which may find instant relief in beneficent action. If there were no remedy for any of these things, to sigh would be a useless

sentimentality. Scripture has nothing but rough scorn for mere fantastic melancholy. Human sorrow is a field too sacred to be abandoned to fine people, .

> "The sluggard Pity's vision-weaving tribe,
> Who sigh for wretchedness, yet shun the wretched,
> Nursing, in some delicious solitude,
> Their slothful loves and dainty sympathies."

No! if Scripture ever forces us, amid our idle chorus, to pause and listen to the sad music of humanity, it is only that it may stir us up the next moment as with a trumpet-blast to active service. In one sense, indeed, there is no remedy against these disturbing elements in the life of man; no armour against fate. No toil of ours can make of this world a safe or perfect place. It is not the hand of man that can ever wipe all tears from off all faces. This fatal flaw in the world that now is, has been recognised by the earliest ages of mankind. It is the Tree of the knowledge of evil which casts its dark shadow even in the Paradise of God. The oldest Epics recognised the truth. Achilles cannot be quite invulnerable in the *Iliad*, nor Siegfried in the *Nibelungen*, nor Balder in the *Eddas*. No stately pleasure house will exclude the gliding phantoms. The arrows of calamity fly in ten thousand different directions, and the air is full of them, and they wound us in the one weak place. Our strength must fail. Our youth must vanish like the morning dew. Our joys must make themselves wings and fly away. Our intellect must grow feebler, our mortal powers decay, our dearest die. "To each his suffering; all are men condemned alike to groan." But what is the lesson? *Not* unmanly complaining; *not* idle speculation; *not* the selfish attempt to secure ourselves alone;—No! but help; no! but sympathy. Not ignorant of misery, we learn, or ought to learn, to help the miserable. Our Lord looked up to Heaven indeed and sighed, because He was a High Priest who can be touched with the feeling of our infirmities; but the sorrow which wrung that sigh from Him did but make Him more earnest day by day in doing good. "The spirit of the Lord is upon me," He said, "because He hath anointed me to preach the gospel to the poor; He has sent me to heal the broken-hearted, to preach deliverance to the captives, and recovering of sight to the blind, to set at liberty them that are bruised." His was no feeble sympathy, but an active ministration. "*I will, be thou clean.*" "*Fear not; only believe.*" "*Take up thy bed, and walk.*" "*Courage, daughter.*" "*Go in peace.*" "*Young man, arise.*" "*Little maid, arise.*" "*Lazarus, come forth.*" "*Go, and sin no more.*"—Such were the arrows of lightnings which He was ever hurling into the mirky air,—such the mighty words that expelled the demon; that cleansed the leper; that nerved the paralytic; that cheered the trembling woman; that gave hope to the despairing sinner; that thrilled into the awful gloom of death. Think of that Sabbath evening at Capernaum, when, as the sunset dyed the silver lake, the people came to Him, bringing with them their demoniacs and their diseased, and far into the deepening dusk, hushing the screams of madness, laying on each tortured sufferer His pure and healing hand, He moved among them; and, though the sighs and groans of all that collective misery smote so sadly upon His heart, yet "He bore our griefs and carried our sorrows," longing only to heal, and save, and bless. My brethren, what a divine example, what a stimulus, what an encouragement, have we here! Our Lord saw all the sorrow; He did not ignore it; He sighed for it; He wept for it; He prayed for it;—but not for one moment did He despair of it;—nay, He worked to lighten it, leaving us thereby, as in all things, an ensample that we should follow His steps.

6. And, thank God, since then, some, in all ages, *have* followed His steps. Some who seem born to it—great souls, like Moses, Samuel, Paul, Francis of Assisi, Xavier, Howard—who from the first choose rather to suffer affliction with the people of God than enjoy the

riches and pleasures of Egypt; others, who, like many of the Apostles, and philanthropists, and missionaries, are called from the fisher's net, or the receipt of customs, or the shop, or the workman's stall, and who obey the calling. Thank God, in spite of all the callousness that does not help, and all the meanness which will not give, the general heart of the world is, I do think, growing more tender. You know the poem about that "woman of a thousand summers back," wife to the grim earl who so taxed his town that the mothers brought their children, clamouring, "If we pay, we starve!"—how

> "She sought her lord . . . . She told him of their tears,
> And prayed him, 'If they pay this tax, they starve.'
> Whereat he stared, replying, half amazed,
> 'You would not let your little finger ache
> For such as *these?*'—'But I would die,' said she.
> He laugh'd, and swore by Peter and by Paul:
> Then fillip'd at the diamond in her ear;
> 'O ay, ay, ay, you talk!'—'Alas!' she said,
> 'But prove me what it is I would not do.'"

Aye and many (and perhaps especially women) have been ready gladly to sacrifice everything to do some good ; to heal, were it ever so little of the world's sorrow. My friends, we have just lost such a one among us here. Mary Stanley was one who delighted to spend and be spent in the service of others. In the days of the Crimean War she was one of that devoted band of ladies who—not afraid of fever or hardship, braving the black Euxine and the bitter cold—went to nurse the sick soldiers in the hospital at Koulalee. But even from her early youth she had devoted herself to teach the children of the poor, and the efforts of her later days to feed the hungry, and warm the shivering, and clothe the naked, and brighten squalid cellars and garrets with the poetry of God's flowers, will long be remembered. And, my friends, the kindly deeds of this life, of every life which has trodden in the warm footsteps of our Saviour through this world's dinted snow, have had their mainspring in that sympathy which was expressed by the sigh of Jesus. We cannot all do as He did in the brief years of His Ministry,—"*go about* doing good"; but we can all live as He lived for His first thirty years of quiet, holy, strenuous duty, deliberately striving each day to *be* good; deliberately striving each day to *do* good; deliberately striving each day to abstain from evil, in order, so far as in us lies, in His name, and for His sake, to assuage the sorrows of the world.

7. Do you ask me how? If you ask me, you can hardly be in earnest. It is like the lawyer's question, "Who is my neighbour?" *Solvitur ambulando.* Your question will answer itself by action. They who are resolutely in earnest to do good do not go about asking, "What good can I do?" they *do it;* they hardly think of it as good; they say "Lord, when did we comfort, when did we visit, when did we feed or clothe Thee?" Why, even a little child at home, even a young boy at school, can do the work of Jesus, and for Jesus. The little child can make home brighter by sweet obedience and glad unselfishness; the young boy can make school nobler by pure

words and faithful deeds. Ah, you cannot do it, if you too do not feel for all the sadness round you; you cannot do it if, in greed, or lust, or selfishness, you are adding to that misery. You cannot make men's temptation less, if all your life long you are swelling the sum of them. You are a mere hypocrite if you pretend to sigh for human sin or human sorrow, while you are ruining souls by your impurity, or defrauding them for your gain. Of some ways in which we can show our share in the sympathy of our Saviour, I may speak hereafter; but ah! if you be sincere, do not wait to have your philanthropy furbished up with appeals for Christmas charities, but go out and be kind, try to do good, try to make the world happier at once:—begin at once, and begin at the very lowest step.

i. There is the animal world, for instance. A mystery it is, a mystery it will ever be. Yet there too we have our work for Jesus. We have abused, alas, too often to purposes of cruelty and tyranny the empire which God granted us over the brutes. It is sad that man has thus made even the most beautiful and innocent part of the animal creation shun, and hate, and fear him. It is not naturally so. In the wilderness Jesus was with the wild beasts, and they harmed Him not. The timid things of the wilderness learnt to trust the ancient hermits. In desert islands the denizens of the forest and the fell shrink not from man until he has shown them his deadliness and treachery. The birds, it is said, and I can well believe it, fluttered without fear about St. Francis of Assisi. For Jesus' sake we have a plain duty to the dumb animals, to be considerate to them, to be gentle with them, to discourage and to abhor all needless cruelty towards them, to teach our boys and our ignorant men to be kind to them, to determine

> "Never to mix our pleasure or our pride
> With sorrow of the meanest thing that feels."

We might learn in this respect even from those who had not heard the divine lessons of the Sermon on the Mount. "A calf destined for sacrifice," we are told in the *Talmud*, put its head, moaning, into the lap of Rabbi Judah the Holy, and he repelled it with the remark, "Go hence; for this thou wast created." "Lo!" said the Angels, "he is pitiless; let affliction come upon him." Again, one day it happened that, in sweeping the room, his maidservant disturbed some young kittens. "Leave them alone," said Rabbi,[1] "for it is written, 'His tender mercies are over all His works.'"[2] Then said the Angels, "Let us have pity on him; for lo! he has learnt pity."[3] And how exquisite is the story which tells us that when Moses was a shepherd in Midian a little lamb left the flock and went frisking into the wilderness; and Moses followed it over rocks and through briers till he had recovered it, and then laying it in his bosom he said, "Little

---

[1] Rabi Judah Hakkodesh, the compiler of the Mishna, is called "Rabbi" *par excellence.*

[2] Ps. cxlv. 9.

[3] Bava Metzia, f. 85. 1. In the original it is not "the Angels," but the indefinite "they" ("They said," אמרי). Comp. Luke xii. 20 (Greek) and xvi. 9.

lamb, thou knowest not what is good for thee; trust me, thy shepherd, and I will guide thee right." And when God saw his tenderness to the straying lamb, He said, "Thou shalt be the shepherd of my people Israel." Might not the old Rabbis teach us the lesson so exquisitely taught us by our own poet in the *Ancient Mariner*, that

> "He prayeth well who loveth well
> Both man, and bird, and beast.
> He prayeth best who loveth best
> All things, both great and small,
> For the dear God who loveth us
> He made and loveth all." [1]

ii. And there is the world of sickness and pain;—but how infinitely is it alleviated by human care, by human skill, by human sympathy, because everywhere, like white-winged

---

[1] We are sometimes apt to flatter ourselves that such sentiments as those illustrated by the *Ancient Mariner* and Wordsworth's *Heart-leap Well* are peculiarly modern; but the Jews (*e.g.* Abarbanel) found them in many parts of the Pentateuch (*e.g.* Ex. xxiii. 4, Lev. xxii. 28, Deut. xxv. 4, xxii. 10, v. 14), and especially in the thrice-repeated command, "Thou shalt not seethe a kid in its mother's milk" (Ex. xxiii. 19, xxxiv. 26, Deut. xiv. 21).

ministers of mercy, the children of God move in and out in the midst of it, healing its ravages, smoothing the sleepless pillow, cooling the fevered brow, shining down upon the suffering with looks and smiles which are a healing in themselves. And we, if we cannot do all this, if we are not good enough to do it, not gifted enough to do it,—too cold, too vulgar, too grasping, too impure to do it,—yet we can help those who are doing it, and love to do it, and we can help at least by our poor gifts to render their efforts possible.

iii. And there is the world of sorrow; and though it must continue while time lasts, there is not one of us who cannot help to make it *less* sorrowful. We can do so passively by abstaining from all churlish deeds and all false and cruel words. We can do so actively by the constant endeavour to cultivate every gentle and kindly feeling, to rejoice with them that do rejoice, and weep with them that weep.

We can do so both actively and passively by the strenuous determination to be kind to many, to wish to be kind to all, willingly to do injury to none. "Be ye kind one to another, tender-hearted, forgiving one another, even as God in Christ forgave you."[1]

Begin with this: of more we may speak another day, but begin with this. This we can all do. All this let us do, and, if often in doing it, we shall have to sigh as Jesus sighed, we shall find that, however the world may treat us, He will also grant to us to become "partakers of His vision and His Sabbath," to share in the infinitude of His peacefulness, to enter into His boundless joy.

---

[1] ὁ Θεὸς ἐν Χριστῷ ἐχαρίσατο ὑμῖν. The rendering of the English version—"*for Christ's sake*"—is here quite indefensible. Comp. 2 Cor. v. 19.

SERMON II.

SINCERITY OF HEART.

THE CONDITION OF TRUE SERVICE FOR THE AMELIORATION OF THE WORLD.

"Nemo malus felix."—Juv. *Sat.* iv..7.

SINCERITY OF HEART AS THE FIRST CONDITION OF SERVICE.

"My beloved are sinking in the sea, and thou art making long prayers," said the Holy One—blessed be He—to Moses. "What then shall I do?" he asked. The Lord said unto Moses, "Speak unto the children of Israel that they go forward (Ex. xiv. 15)."—Sotah, *f.* 37, 1.

Πρᾶξις ἐπίβασις Θεωρίας, GREG. NAZ.

Συνεργοῦντες δέ, 2 Cor. vi. 1.

Θεοῦ γάρ ἐσμεν συνεργοί, 1 Cor. iii. 9.

τοῦ Κυρίου συνεργοῦντος, Mark xvi. 20.

Almighty and merciful God, of whose only gift it cometh that Thy faithful people do unto Thee true and laudable service, grant, we beseech Thee, that we may so faithfully serve Thee in this life that we fail not finally to attain Thy heavenly promises, through the merits of Jesus Christ our Lord. Amen.

SERMON II.

SINCERITY OF HEART AS THE FIRST CONDITION OF SERVICE.

LUKE XXII. 32.

"*And when thou art converted, strengthen thy brethren.*"[1]

WE spoke, my friends, last Sunday of the sigh of Jesus before He healed the blind man and said Ephphatha, "Be opened." We saw that it was a sigh heaved over the miseries of a world in ruins. We forced ourselves to notice the truth that there is a deep crack and flaw in

---

[1] A more literal rendering would be "when once thou hast turned again." Some commentators make the word ἐπιστρέψας little more than an expletive (comp. Ps. lxxxiv. 6; Acts vii. 42), "thou in thy turn" (*vicissim*). But the English version is correct. The word is here used intransitively, as in Matt. xiii. 15 (in its physical sense), and in Acts xvi. 18, Rev. i. 12; it is used transitively in Luke i. 16, Acts xxvii. 18, James v. 19.

this material universe; that in the unintelligent creation, in the animal kingdom, in the world of man, there has occurred some terrible disaster and convulsion, of which the effects are not wholly by us remediable; but of which we hope that the traces will be finally obliterated at the restitution of all things,[1] and of which, by a mystery which we cannot understand, the amelioration is left in large measure in the hands of man. On the possibilities and methods of that amelioration we did but touch, because my object then was simply to bring before you a fact which, from the equable pressure of its universal incidence, we are often content to ignore, or which, to the best of our power, we energetically strive to avert from ourselves, while with fatal selfishness we acquiesce in it for others. But if this prevalence of evil be the most awful fact of human life, it is one which we should keep constantly before us, not as a cause of depression, still

---

[1] Ἄχρι χρόνων ἀποκαταστάσεως πάντων, Acts iii. 21; ἐν τῇ παλιγγενεσίᾳ, Matt. xix. 28.

less as an excuse for inaction and despair, but as a stimulus to self-denying duty, and as an exercise of noble faith. We saw that not once or twice only in this life our Saviour sighed, and wept, and groaned deeply in spirit. And how could He do otherwise than sigh, as He looked upon the planks and broken fragments and shattered hulks which strew the tossing sea of life, and which tell of the utter shipwreck of so many gallant barques? Yet His was no sigh of idle and useless pity. It was no mere sign that He too suffered with those whom He saw suffer. He did not, as St. Augustine says, merely stand upon the shore, while we are toiling amid the troubled waves; nay, but He came to us walking across the stormy waters; He entered into our tossing ship, and calmed the tempest, and brought us to the haven where we would be.[1] He sighed, but it was only as He trod the hard path of our deliverance; only as *pertransivit benefaciendo*, "He passed through the world doing good." We

[1] John vi. 21.

may sigh too; we can hardly choose but sigh at times; and, if the sigh be noble and sincere, then

> "Never a sigh of passion or of pity,
>   Never a wail for weakness or for wrong,
>   Has not its archive in the angels' city,
>   Finds not its echo in the endless song."

But the sigh should be as it were but the transient safety-valve of some exceptional emotion; whereas the active kindness, the efficient energy, should be the solemn and sacred work of life. Alas! my friends, we can do but little. Our faculties are very limited, very partial. The gifts of even the most gifted of us are few and one-sided. Even when we are most wishing and trying to be faithful, we are at the best but unprofitable servants.[1] Our achievements lag perpetually far behind our ideal; and the hinder wheel can as little overtake the fore

---

[1] Luke xvii. 10, ἀχρεῖοι, "insufficient," "unmeritorious" (Rom. iii. 12); "inutiles, insufficientes quia nemo tantum timet, tantum diligit, tantum credit Deo, quantum oportet."—AUG. *Conf.*

wheel of a chariot, as our endeavours can overtake our sense of duty.[1] But yet on the one hand the *fact* is clear, that this world is very sinful and very sorrowful; and the *duty* is clear—" Strive to make it better ;" and the *command* is clear—" Take thou thy individual share in this work of healing ;" and the individual *promise* is clear—" Not a cup of cold water given in Christ's name to Christ's little ones shall miss of its reward ; " and the universal *fulfilment* of the promise is clear—that God has ever blessed with fruitfulness the honest labour of those who have laboured in His cause. And so in all hours of despondency, of self-reproach, of failing power, of efforts miserably unsuccessful, of means obviously disproportionate, of opposition apparently overwhelming, the whisper comes to us, Duties are thine ; results are God's. See only that thine intent be good and pure, and the event

[1] " Nam quamvis prope te, quamvis temone sub uno
  Vertentem sese, frustra sectabere canthum
  Cum rota posterior curras et in axe secundo."
        —Pers. *Sat.* v. 70-72.

thou mayest safely leave in the hands of God.

This then is the only thing which every Christian, every good man, has to bear in mind—that he ought to "deal courageously, and then the Lord shall be with the good."[1] God gives thee the high privilege of being a fellow labourer with Him.[2] Do not be troubled if, in spite of all that thou triest to do, the times are out of joint, and things go wrong, and thou seemest to do no good. God made the world, not thou. He has patience; shouldest not thou have patience? Even thy poor good deeds cannot die. If they seem at first to yield no fruit, they shall still be as seeds shut up in the darkness of a sepulchre, and when they are taken from the dead hand of time, years afterwards, it may be, they shall rise in golden grain. Be it little, be it much, God will accept thy honest offering. Better than the holocausts of the wicked shall be the fragment of bread given to the world's hunger, or the grain of salt flung into its corruption. For—

[1] 2 Cor. vi. 1. [2] 2 Chron. xix. 11

> "God doth not need
> Either our work, or His own gifts; who best
> Bear His mild yoke, they serve Him best. His state
> Is kingly; thousands at His bidding speed,
> And post o'er land and ocean without rest;
> They also serve who only stand and wait."

In this world of sin and sorrow then we have work to do, and the question is, What work, and how can we do it? Let us take this afternoon the World of Sin, and plainly, practically, with earnest consideration, above all asking the blessing of the Holy Spirit of God, let us consider whether we can do anything; and what we can, what we ought to do. On all sides of us we see life blighted and ruined by human passions, which sweep over it like flame over a dry heath, and leave it black and scarred behind them. The sorrows of the world are in the main the heritage of its sins, and these bitter fruits of sin have their bitter roots in selfishness. We can do nothing till we have clearly recognised the conditions which we have to face. Only look then with me at the plain facts which are so palpable to every clear vision in the world around us.

1. Look, for instance, at Intemperance. Merely draw the circle of a far bowshot round this Abbey, and I could take you to house after house, and tell you of tragedy after tragedy, from this cause alone. Every case to which I allude shall be an actual, not an imaginary case—a case which I have personally visited, not one of which I have merely heard. In *this* house—if these wretched and filthy tenements can be called houses—is a miserable mother wounded by the drunken assault of her own son. There is a husband who has been imprisoned for brutality to his own wife. There a poor honest woman whose husband felled her to the earth when she came to entreat him not to waste his scant earnings in the reeking gin-shop. There a young woman only snatched from suicide to plunge into fresh excesses, almost as soon as her life had been restored. Here a young man the curse and shame of all his family. There a poor lone woman frightened into imbecility by a drunken lodger. There a family starved and shivering,

while week by week the man squanders his wages in tipsy riot over the bar of the public house. I tell you that within a bowshot of this Abbey I could take you to these sufferers, and show you many, many more. There are crowded streets in which I have known such cases in almost every house. And however much you may try to persuade yourselves, and let others persuade you, that intemperance is not the deadly curse of England, you know in your hearts as well as I do—or with the smallest possible expenditure of trouble in examining the evidence you *may* know—that all this, and much more than this, comes from the multiplied and unrestricted sale of that which, to myriads of a vitiated population, acts as a strong poison and a besetting curse. And now extend the circle; multiply these miseries of one single parish ten thousand fold; let them be spread over colonies and continents in widening zones of ruin and temptation; and there you have one phase of the work of one deadly evil spirit in England and in the world. And the voice of God says to us, says to *thee*—*Is it nothing to you, all ye that pass by?*

2. Or look at Impurity. It is a subject which must be lightly handled, for in its very name is contamination, and there is pestilence in its most distant breath. A young man, in the degraded impulse of passions,—which, when uncontrolled, debase man not only *to* the level, but *below* the level of the beasts that perish,— wrongs the faith, or betrays the weakness which trusted him. It is his *pleasure;* and what comes of his infamous pleasure thus recklessly and selfishly indulged? For him, if he repent, agonies of shame; and burdens of remorse; and, it may be, years of guilty consequence: if he repent *not*, and if—which is far worse for him—he seems to go unpunished, a callous heart, and a fearful looking for, and a curse watching his life with hungry eyes, and finally that certain retribution which comes, and must come, now or hereafter, on all unrepented sin. That is the result for *him*. And what for the victim of his crime? For *her*, a blighted

life, a ruined home, a seared heart, the anguish of those who loved her, the beginning it may be of such shame as—so far at any rate as this world is concerned—had made it better for her if she had not been born. That is one form of impurity; one only of its many forms. Multiply it by millions, with all its resultant horrors of loathly sickness; of ruined intellect; of sapped strength; of hidden shame; of homes made like hell; of minds smouldering with the inward torture of unhallowed fire; of lives whose root is as rottenness, and their blossom is gone up as dust; and there you see the work of *another* demon from the abyss, sent forth by the Powers of Darkness to plague mankind. And once more that voice of God says to us, says to *thee—Is it nothing to you, all ye that pass by?*

3. Or look at Hatred, its rarer active forms of murder, assault, violence, cruelty; its more universal, and in their aggregate hardly less injurious forms of envy, spite, scandal, uncharitableness, innuendo, depreciation, slander,

malice, whispering, backbiting—multiform developments of one base passion, multiform names for one base thing. Thousands of men, for instance, get their living by writing anonymously. The anonymous is to them an invisible ring whereby they can, with impunity, often even unsuspected, speak of others all words that may do hurt. It is as an impregnable shield, from behind whose shelter they can shower arrow-flights of falsehoods, sneers, misrepresentations, disparagements at their defenceless victims. They can tarnish the merits of an opponent. They can obliterate the services of a rival. They can gild the follies of a partisan. They can secretly blight the hopes of a nominal friend. They can give a false aspect to fair reasonings, a foolish appearance to just opinions. They can sneer away honest reputations, and push empty pretensions into prominence. They can abuse the good, and belaud the bad. They can be as false, as hollow, as malignant as many such writers daily show themselves to be. There are, of course, many who nobly resist these temptations. They can wear the mask without using the dagger. But the number is not too large of those who can show the supreme virtue of thus being able to wear this ring of Gyges[1] and of never abusing it to base purposes. In the London press, and in the local press, and even, alas! in the so-called "religious" press, anonymity is open to the basest of mankind; and even when names are signed there is an ample sphere for conceit and Pharisaism; and malice is relished; and lies are profitable; and bad men can let their tongues "rage like a fire against the noblest names;" and the many-headed beast of credulity, ignorance, and envy accepts what they say. "Their throat is an open sepulchre; with their tongues have they deceived; the poison of asps is under their lips."[2] And thus, alike in public life and in private life, does

---

[1] Plat. *Rep.* ii. § 3; Herod. i. 8. Hence the proverb Γύγου δακτύλιον. "Hunc igitur ipsum annulum si habeat sapiens nihilo plus sibi licere putet peccare, quam si non haberet Honesta enim bonis viris non occulta quaeruntur."—CIC. *de Off.* iii. 9

[2] Rom iii. 13, 14; Ps. v. 9; Matt. xv. 18, 19; Ja. v. 2-8; i. 26.

the innate baseness and littleness of the corrupted human heart shoot out its arrows—even bitter words. And in a world where David once said in his haste that "All men are liars," and where even good men have been sometimes tempted to say the same thing at their leisure, the voice of God asks us, asks *thee—Is it nothing to you, all ye that pass by ?*

4. Once more,—for I shall not attempt to exhaust the catalogue, or fill in the outlines of the unlovely picture—look at the love of money. It is a fiend—this Mammon [1]—which tries to wear a more respectable exterior than other fiends. He goes to church, and figures not seldom in the phylacteries of the Pharisee. Yet, this is he who taints with falsity so much of the trade and commerce of the world. Who that is familiar with all the ins and outs of "business" has not heard of false balances; deceitful weights; sham prices; exorbitant demands;

---

[1] The personification is of course later. The word is a substantive, derived perhaps from אָמַן. "De mammonâ—de *nummo* scilicet."—TERT. *adv. Marc.* iv. 33.

adulterated goods; the bribing of household servants; the rings of middlemen to prey on the community; deliberate combinations to keep up artificial prices; good dealers made to pay bad debts; "trade customs," which, if they were not regarded as customs, would be regarded as plain dishonesties? Who has not heard of—perhaps suffered from—swindling speculations, bubble companies, fraudulent bankrupts, defaulting trustees, cunning embezzlements, pious directors of unstable banks? Who does not see grasping luxury, which will not stretch out one of its fingers to the grinding poverty at its very doors?—Who does not know of "Wealth, a monster gorged, mid starving populations"? All these are the result of that universal love of money, which is the root of all evil; they are the works of Mammon,

> "Mammon, the least erected spirit that fell
> From heaven; for even in heaven his looks and thoughts
> Were ever downward bent, admiring more
> The riches of heaven's pavement, trodden gold,
> Than aught divine or holy else enjoyed
> In vision beatific."

And when you look over this dreary waste of avarice,—when you see myriads loving not God but gold—says not the voice of God again to *thee*—*Is it nothing to you, all ye that pass by?*

5. Well, my brethren, these are some of the phenomena of the world we live in; some of the conditions which exist around us and which we strive hardest to ignore. But things are, as they are; and *this* is the World of Sin. We may not leave it. It were treason in these days to fly from it to the monastery or to the hermitage. We live in the midst of it, and it is in vain merely to cry "Woe is me that I am constrained to dwell with Mesech, and to have my habitation among the tents of Kedar." We are where God has placed us, and there we must stay till He gives us the signal to fall out of the ranks. Let us recognise these plain facts. I feel well assured that if you would think of it, and confess it, there is not one among all you who hear me who has not been painfully grazed, in the lives of those dear

to you, or sorely wounded, in your own lives, by the poisoned barbs of one or other of these sins of lust, or excess, or slander, or hate, or avarice. And these were among the worst miseries which made Jesus sigh. *He* too had seen all these things. We saw last Sunday that He was familiar with the world of sorrow; He was no less familiar with the world of sin. He had lived for thirty years in a malignant, gossiping provincial village. He had seen an evil and adulterous generation. He had suffered from slanderous Pharisees and sneering Sadducees. He had seen depraved sinners, and cheating publicans. He had watched the highly respected Dives, in his luxury and selfishness, with sycophants fawning on him at the banquet, while Lazarus lay starving and dying at his gates. He had seen the rich niggard striding selfishly about his barns, while the poor were dying out of doors. He had seen the gay young fool ride away from the home of his father to "see life," as he called it, and "enjoy himself." He had seen him devour his living with harlots; He had seen him famishing among the swine. And all these things "stuck in Him like a nail." But was He content to see this, and only *pity* it? Nay, but He did all that His very utmost love could do. For the sake of these hard Pharisees, and niggardly misers, and lying critics, and gay young fools—and all their conceit and misery, and all their hardness and malignity, and all their weakness and shame, He left heaven; He emptied Himself of His glory; He took on Him a slave's semblance; He chose the poor man's lot. He left the high Hallelujahs of the Seraphim for the weeping and gnashing of teeth of this world's outer darkness. He shrank not from shuddering contact with its leprosy of meanness, and lust, and hate.—He not only *sighed* for the world;—He *died* for it, amid the execrations of its howling multitudes, upon its cross of agonising shame!

6. And He did all this to redeem the world; and it was part of His work of redemption to leave *us* to fill up what was lacking in His

afflictions; to render it possible for us to do the work which He gave us to do.[1] We need not (as I have said already) try to fathom the mystery *why* God should require, should demand, should reward the agency of man; why instead of enlightening the heathen He should bid *us* enlighten the heathen; why He should bid *us*—miserable, faithless creatures that we are—bid *us* feed His lambs; bid *us* comfort His afflicted; bid *us* set free His prisoners; bid *us* take care of His poor. It is useless for us to ask *why* it is so; suffice us that it *is* so. What then are we to do? Refuse His command we cannot, for we are His children, His soldiers, His scholars, His servants. What then are we to do?—How can we make better His ruined world of sin?

7. Well, my brethren, the first answer—the only one on which we can dwell to-day—is a very

---

[1] Col. i. 24. On what is meant by supplementing the deficiencies of the afflictions of Christ, not by *vicarious* but by *ministrative* and *useful* sufferings, I may refer to my *Life of St. Paul*, ii. 458.

simple one. But, though simple, it is stringent, rigid, and inexorable. It is that we can only begin to do Christ's work, in striving to make His world better, by *personal innocence*, by *personal holiness*. Ah, how many will stumble over this entrance! The priests of Dagon used to leap over the threshold of their idol;[1] but not so can any one enter into the Temple of the Most High God. The way into that temple shall be called the way of holiness.[2] The man who is not sincere in self-amelioration can never be a prophet of God. Men who have begun wickedly have indeed sometimes—like St. Augustine, like Bunyan, like Whitefield—turned over a new leaf, and begun a new life. But I do not believe that even these—greatly as God blessed their efforts—have done as much as they other-

[1] See Zeph. i. 9. "In the same day also will I punish all those that leap on the threshold." Kimchi explains this of those who forcibly enter the dwellings of the poor; but the passage is usually explained by a custom of the priests of Dagon, who are said to have leaped over the threshold on which the Fish-god's head and hands were broken (1 Sam. v. 5). This seems to be the view of the Chaldee Paraphrast.

[2] Is. xxxv. 8.

wise might have done. For surely that man builds better who builds upon foundations than he who builds on ruins. And this at any rate is certain, that no hypocrite, no bad, no insincere man, can heal in any degree the sinfulness of the world. Not till he is converted, can he strengthen his brethren. Alas! even when he *is* converted, he may find that he has maimed, that he has ruined his own transcendent powers of usefulness. How bitter was the wail of the mighty Mirabeau, that if he had had but character, if he had but been a pure and righteous man, if he had not degraded his life by sensuality, and his youth by evil passions, he could have saved France. Many a man has felt the same. He has clipt his own wings; he has suffered to be shorn away the sunny locks of the Nazarite, wherein would have lain his strength; he has wounded himself; and even when the wound has closed, the frightful scar remains. But if, while he himself is still in the gall of bitterness and the bond of iniquity, he essays to amend the morals of the world, he

F

will either disgrace and weaken his own cause, or the good he does in one direction will be undone by the evil in the other. To such an one—shaming him, weakening him, warning him that they who bear the vessels of the sanctuary must themselves be clean [1]—come the stern words of Christ, "First cast out the beam out of thine own eye, and then shalt thou see clearly to take out the mote out of thy brother's eye;" [2]—or the crushing questions with which St. Paul suddenly beats down the self-satisfied boast of the Pharisees—"Thou makest thy pillow on the law; and boastest in God; and dost recognise His will; and dost discriminate the transcendent; and art confident that thyself art a leader of the blind, a light of those in darkness, a trainer of the foolish, a teacher of babes—thou then that teachest another, teachest thou not thyself?

---

[1] Is. lii. 11.

[2] Matt. vii. 5. The English version here misses the distinction of the ἐκ and the ἀπό, which is the best reading, in v. 4. The mote is only on the surface of our brother's eye; the beam is in the depths of our own.

Thou that proclaimest not to steal, dost thou steal? thou that sayest do not commit adultery, dost thou commit adultery? loather of idols, dost thou rob temples? thou who boastest in the law, through transgression of the law dost thou dishonour God?"[1] As in the words of the modern poet—

> "Thou to wax fierce
>   In the cause of the Lord,
> To threat and to pierce
>   With the heavenly sword!
> Thou warnest and smitest;
>   Yet Christ must atone
> For a soul which thou slightest—
>   Thine own."[2]

8. Yes, my brethren, let us understand it very distinctly—understand it as an eternal and inevitable condition—that to *do* good, we must *be* good. When any one is a truly good man, then even if he takes no part whatever in holy wars against the sin of the world, his mere

---

[1] For the reasons of various expressions in this translation of Rom. ii. 17-23, I must refer to my *Life of St Paul*, ii. 201, 202.

[2] J. H. Newman, *Poems*.

unconscious influence, his mere passive character becomes a blessing to others, and without any conscious endeavour he still drops his little quota into the stream of the world's improvement. About the mere presence and person of good men there hangs a charm and spell of good which makes them do good, even when they are not consciously thinking of good. Their very face does good, as though it were the face of an angel, and from their mere silence there spreads an influence—a "flowing in"—of higher motives, and purer thoughts into the souls of men. It was said of the ancient Cato that, when he entered, the young Roman nobles blushed for their base amusements. It is told of the young Bernadino of Siena that, even as a boy, all bad words were hushed at once when he joined a group of his companions.[1] And so too the mere presence of bad men makes us bad. Marguerite asks Faust with surprise how it is that she finds herself unable

---

[1] Mrs. Jameson, *Art Legends of the Monastic Orders*, p. 291.

to pray when his friend is with him.[1] How many a crime has been consummated solely because of vicious weakness unconsciously made plastic by the voiceless power of stronger wickedness! Among the pure and good, the base and impure inspire a shuddering repulsion, such as the presence of Judas Iscariot seems to have inspired in the heart of St. John; but among the many who are but weakly bad, the contagion of stronger wickedness has an assimilating force. How many might say with the guilty king—

> "Hadst not thou been by,
> A fellow by the hand of nature sealed,
> Quoted, and signed, to do a deed of shame,
> This murther had not come into my mind. . . .
> Hadst thou but shook thy head, or made a pause,
> Or turned an eye of doubt upon my face,
> As bid me tell my tale in express words,
> Deep shame had struck me dumb, made me break off,

---

[1] "Das übermannt mich so mehr,
Dass wo er [Mephistopheles] nur mag zu uns treten,
Mein ich sogar ich liebte dich nicht mehr.
Auch wenn er da ist, könnt' ich nimmer beten,
Und das frisst mir ins Herz hinein."
—GOETHE, *Faust*.

And those thy fears might have wrought fears in me;
But thou didst understand me by my signs,
And didst in signs again parley with sin;
Yea, without stop, didst let thy heart consent,
And consequently thy rude hand to act,
The deed which both our tongues held vile to name."[1]

And so, when bad men are *not* yet hardened in wickedness they can be won over by the good, but, when they are, they hate and persecute the good whose mere silent lives rebuke them. It was thus that Sodom hated Lot. It was thus that the Ephesians expelled Hermodorus because he was virtuous.[2] It was thus that the Athenians ostracised Aristides because he was just. "The honourable and *religious* gentleman," said a slave-holding member of parliament, speaking of Wilberforce in the House of Commons; and he was properly scathed in reply with the lightnings of that good man's eloquence. But the epithet spoke volumes for the silent, the unconscious, the inevitable *influence*,—the silent, the unconscious

---

[1] *King John*, act. iv. sc. 2.
[2] Diog. Laert. ix. 2; Cic. *Tusc. Disp.* v. 36.

rebuke of vice, and protest for holiness which springs from the ordinary life of every true and righteous man. And mark that when the bad, hating the good, sneer them out of court, repress them by violence, madden the blind multitude against them with dark lies, poison them as Socrates was poisoned, banish them as Epictetus was banished, burn them as Savonarola was burned, execrate them as Whitefield was execrated, do not think that then the good have failed. "Even in their ashes live their wonted fires;" their voices even from the grave sound in the thunder's mouth; their dead hands pull down the strongholds of their enemies, and tyrants tremble at their ghosts. What was the end of Jesus? Between two murderers He hung in agony upon His cross, amid the howlings alike of secular, and of religious, hate; and, before three centuries were over, that gibbet of torture and of infamy sat upon the sceptres and shone in the crowns of kings.

9. Be this much then, dear brethren, our

lesson to-day. Are we mere base, sensual, frivolous, greedy, grasping creatures?—the mere "hungers, thirsts, fevers, appetites," money-makers and money-investors of the world?—creeping about amid the low noises of the mist, and caring only to clutch such husks as we may find?—Are we this (and alas! it would describe too many lives!)—or are we noble enough to enter into the meaning of the sigh of Jesus, and share His pure and divine compassion for the world? Well, if so, we must also enter into the spirit of His life. And the very first condition of doing that is sincerity;—a sincerity which can only be shown in the whole-hearted effort after personal innocence, after personal holiness. It is to *this* point that my whole appeal, and my whole argument, has tended. If we would do as Jesus did, we must be His servants. If we would help to heal the evils of the world, we must ourselves be free from them. If we would tend the plague-stricken, there must not be the plague in our own hearts. We must be consistent, and give proofs of our consistency

It was in vain for Seneca to declaim against luxury in villas which excited the envy of an emperor; or against greed with millions out at extortionate usury. Such declamations sound hollow; such appeals ring false. He who would help others, must not only show the way, but lead the way.

If, for instance, we would heal the woes inflicted by *Intemperance*, let us beware that we are not perishing by permitted things.[1] We shall not reclaim others from excess by going ourselves to the utmost verge of indulgence; nor is it the boon companion who as a rule will rescue the drunkard from his fall.

Again, if we would fain heal the horrible evils caused by *Sensuality*—its inward rottenness—its pervading corruption—its burning intensity—its hardened selfishness—its stealthy contamination: then we must be pure in life; and we must pray more and more, and strive more and more, to be pure in heart. Blessed and happy is he who can show in his own life that the

[1] "*Perimus licitis;*" motto of Sir Matthew Hale.

repression of unlawful impulse is the well-spring of unwonted strength. "Blessed will he be who shall re-persuade the world how divine is the blush of modesty on young human cheeks; how high, beneficent, sternly inexorable, if forgotten, is the duty laid, not on women only, but on every creature, in regard to these particulars."[1]

Again, if we would help to cure the world, and England, and London, and the rich, and the middle classes, and trade, of the cancer of *Greed*, it will be useless if we ourselves are basely and selfishly fond of money. We must ourselves be superior to this dull yellow fascination; we must ourselves be able to pour silent contempt on gold; to have the open hand and the liberal heart; to prove our belief in the truth that it is more blessed to give than to receive; to find our best investments in private acts of charity and public deeds of munificence; to stem, so far as we can, that creeping wave of

---

[1] Carlyle, *Frederic the Great*, ii. 30.

niggardliness which, like the muddy tide on the coast of Lancashire, is "always shallow, yet always just high enough to drown." The threepenny pieces in the offertory plate must no longer be the indication of the organised hypocrisy of our charitableness, and the daring secrecy of our unbelief. We raised statues to an American merchant, because in his lifetime he gave a large sum to the poor, as though he were a hero,—as though the gift of a rich man out of vast superfluity were some phenomenal and unheard-of virtue. Doubtless the rarity of such munificence made it look like an act of antique saintliness; but if such deeds had been so highly thought of in the early days of Christianity there would have been statues in every street. Hundreds of rich men among us might, almost without feeling it, have followed his example if they would have prayed the prayer graved upon the slab, beneath which for a time his body rested in the nave of this Abbey, "My daily prayer to my Heavenly Father was, that in gratitude for the mercies He has granted me, I might be enabled to do some signal good to my fellow creatures before I died."

Lastly, if we desire to heal the deadly wounds of malice, we must look well to it that in our conversation be never heard the serpent's hiss. We must speak no slander, no, nor listen to it. We must not help the half-brained dwarf society—

> "To find low motives unto noble deeds,
> To fix all doubt upon the darker side;"

but our speech must be with grace seasoned with salt. The reputations of our enemies must be as sacred from our gossip as those of our dearest relatives, and the absent must be as safe on our lips from secret malice as are the dead.

10. My brethren, are these hard conditions? They are not too hard if we use the grace which God gives us, and ask for more grace; and they are noble conditions; and they are absolutely indispensable conditions; and they *do*

contribute to the mighty end in view. He who does this,—he who lives thus;—he whose appetites are his slaves, not his masters;—he who has never dropped into the ears of another the "leperous distilment" of unclean thoughts; —he who can give liberally and not grudge;—he whose palm does not itch for gold;—he who can love even his enemies;—he who can not merely *say* "I forgive," but can and does *ex animo* forgive even those who have secretly and most seriously wronged him;—he who keeps innocency, and does the thing that is right, and speaks the truth from his heart, and has not given his money upon usury, nor sworn to deceive his neighbour—*he* shall not only find peace at the last—shall not only receive for himself the blessing of the Lord, and righteousness from the God of his salvation: but men shall take note of him that he has been with Jesus. And however obscure or humble may have been his lot;—however much fools may have counted his life madness, and his end to be without honour;—yet, because he has left the world better than he found it, wisdom at last shall be justified of her children; the judgments of Heaven shall correct the false and partial judgments of man's brief day;[1] the memory of the just shall be blessed, when the name of the wicked rots.

[1] 1 Cor. iv. 3, ἐμοὶ δὲ εἰς ἐλάχιστόν ἐστιν, ἵνα ὑφ' ὑμῶν ἀνακριθῶ ἢ ὑπὸ ἀνθρωπίνης ἡμέρας.

SERMON III.

ENERGY OF CHRISTIAN SERVICE.

ENERGY OF CHRISTIAN SERVICE.

Almighty God, who didst give such grace to Thy holy Apostles that they readily obeyed the calling of Thy Son Jesus Christ, and followed Him without delay, grant unto us all that we, being called by Thy Holy Word, may forthwith give up ourselves obediently to fulfil Thy Holy Commandments, through the same Jesus Christ our Lord. Amen.

ΠΟΛΛΟΙ ΓΑΡ ΕΙΣΙ ΚΛΗΤΟΙ, ΟΛΙΓΟΙ ΔΕ ΕΚΛΕΚΤΟΙ.—Matt. xx. 16.

Μέγας γὰρ ὁ ἀγών· μέγας, καὶ οὐχ ὅσος δοκεῖ· τὸ χρηστὸν ἢ κακὸν γενέσθαι.—PLATO.

εἰσὶ γὰρ δὴ ὥς φασι περὶ τὰς τελετὰς ναρθηκοφόροι μὲν πολλοί, βάκχοι δέ γε παῦ, οι.—CLEM. ALEX. *Strom.* i. p. 315; v. p. 554.

"He's a slave who dare not be
In the right with two or three;
He's a slave who would not choose
Hatred, slander, and abuse,
Rather than in silence shrink
From the truth he needs must think."—J. R. LOWELL.

"What is martyrdom
But death-defying utterance of belief?"—GEORGE ELIOT.

SERMON III.

ENERGY OF CHRISTIAN SERVICE.

MATT. xx. 6, 7

"Why stand ye here all the day idle? Go ye also into the vineyard."

WE were led, my friends, two Sundays ago, to think over the meaning of the sigh of Jesus when He said, "Ephphatha, be opened;" and seeing that it was wrung from Him by deep compassion for a sick and sinful world, we tried to learn how ignoble it would be in us if we did not share that deep compassion, and find in it, as He found in it, a stimulus to noble action. And when, last Sunday, we thought of the ways in which we could each take our humble share in the vast, the necessary, the Christlike work of the amelioration of the world, we saw further that the sorrows of the world are caused mainly by its sins; and that, in the warfare against those sins, the very first condition is sincerity and wholeheartedness in ourselves—the struggle at least after personal innocence and personal holiness. I am speaking to hundreds who are unknown, and who never will be known beyond their own circle, or the parish in which they live; to hundreds who, a few years after their deaths, will be as pathetically forgotten as though the river of Lethe had flowed over their obliterated names. Yet they may be dearer to God than the most famous, and their work as precious to men "as the continuity of the sunbeams is precious," though we forget the brightness of the past summer days. For no mean benefactor of the world is he, who, even in the humblest and most private capacity, has been able to show — were it but by his obscure example in one quiet home—that his soul breathes a purer atmosphere than that which floats in the corrupted currents of the world. "He is a good man," said Napoleon of

Prince Charles of Austria, a general whom he had often met on the field of battle, "*he is a good man, and that is everything.*" Aye, for our own individual peace and blessedness doubtless it is. There is an awful duty incumbent on each one of us to be at least thus much. Alas! how many of us can venture humbly to hope that we are good men? Of how many would all men say with any emphasis of conviction, "He is a good man"? And even of those whom others reckon among the good, how many would be able, even in the lowest sense, to accept such a title for themselves?[1] Amid the storms of the sea of life, its

---

[1] "How few are those whose passage upon this foolish planet has been marked by actions really good and useful! I bow myself to the earth before him of whom it can be said, '*Pertransivit benefaciendo;*' who has succeeded in instructing, consoling, relieving his fellow creatures; who has made real sacrifice for the sake of doing good; those heroes of silent charity who hide themselves and expect nothing in the world. But what are the common run of men like? and how many are there of us in a thousand who can ask themselves without terror, 'What have I done in this world? Wherein have I advanced the general work? and what is left of me for good and for evil?'"—J. DE MAISTRE.

devious currents, its treacherous calms, its sunken reefs, its wreckers' beacons, how many of us are sailing straight to the everlasting haven, with firm hand upon the helm? Ah, it is a great thing, it is "a far cry" to most of us, to be merely good men, victors of our spiritual enemies, victors of ourselves. "It is hard," said the ancient thinker, "a hard struggle, and not so easy as it seems, to become good." He was right. It is a hard thing, and there are thousands of us, it may be, of whom as yet, God asks nothing more.

2. And yet there have been epochs of history, there are crises in all men's lives, in which God does require more; in which He needs the aid not only of His called, who are many, but of His elected, who are few. Let us think this afternoon whether that call does not come *specially* to some;—in its measure to every one of us. It is told of a brave bishop, not long dead, that when he decided to leave all English prospects to face the struggles of a young colony, a very high ecclesiastical dignitary

expressed his intense astonishment that a man so well situated, such a "rising man," to use the vulgar term, should sacrifice all ease and all ambition to go forth to hardship and poverty. "I suppose," said the friend to whom the expression of surprise was addressed, " I suppose that

> " 'He sees a hand you cannot see,
> Which beckons him away;
> He hears a voice you cannot hear
> Which will not let him stay.' "

"Ah!" said the other, wholly unconscious of the covert irony, "I suppose that must be it!" That a young man, marked for what the world calls "promotion" and "success," should actually resign this for a position of no ease and little dignity, was to the good old dignitary an inexplicable enigma. But, my brethren, do we not all of us, at our nobler moments, hear also that voice and summons? Have we not all seen, at times of our clearest vision, the beckoning fingers of that mysterious hand?.

And, if so, *whence* does the hand beckon us?

Far from the world; from its farms and its merchandise; from its conventionality and malice; from its hypocrisies and follies; from its greed and ambition; from its vulgarities of comfort, and surfeitings of luxury; from the jostling, pressing, elbowing crowd of its selfish competitions; from its littlenesses and hatreds; from its vain pomp and show; from its degraded religionism, its rancorous contentions, its vain, vile hopes.

And *whither* does the voice call us? To efforts for Heaven's eternal treasures, rather than for earth's perishing gold; to the sacrifice, if need be, of earthly hopes, of earthly enjoyments, of earthly affections; to names recorded, not on Fame's icy tablets, but in God's book of life; to the rank and promotion, not of them "who have their good things in this life," but of the last here who shall there be first in goodness. Aye, and to goodness for the sake of goodness; to the lessons of the Mountain of Beatitudes; to work for God, not for self, and for the sake of the service not for the sake of the reward. Has not that voice sometimes called us "to Mount Sion, and the spirits of just men made perfect, and to Jesus, the Mediator of the New Covenant, and to the blood of sprinkling, which speaketh better things than the blood of Abel"? Do any of you, were it even in faintest tone, hear that call to-day? Does it say to you, "You are walking in the sacred procession, but do you feel the inspiring God"?[1] Does it ask you, Are you even trying to save your own soul, or are you drowning it in the mud of pleasure and the siftings of gold? And ah! if you are trying to save your own soul, does it content you to save it alone? Is the whole world of "men, your brothers," nothing to you? does the sigh of Jesus wake no echo in your heart? Are you content to clutch for your bare self one plank amid the fiery deluge of universal ruin? Do you think that selfishness for Time is a sin, but that if it be spun out to Eternity it is a Celestial Prudence? Or

---

[1] πολλοί τοι ναρθηκοφόροι βάκχοι δέ τέ ταῦροι.—PLAT. *Phaed.* 69. c.

will you rather cry, "O Lord, let me not live in vain! let me not live only for my own miserable, shivering, hungry self! Thou hast work to do, oh let me do it! Lord! what wouldst Thou have me to do? Here am I, send me!" And even while you pray thus, will you be willing to add with the deep submission of a good man in the last words which he wrote in his diary, "Let me labour to do God's will, yet not anxious that it should be done by me rather than by others if God disapproves of my doing it"?[1] Alas, my friends, how few of us are good enough—how few confident enough in ourselves—how many of us are too "pale in virtue, and faintly dyed in integrity," to speak thus! Yet such men there have been; and surely in this Abbey, if anywhere,

> "Ever their statues rise before us,
>   Our loftier brothers but one in blood;
> At bed and table they lord it o'er us,
>   With looks of beauty and words of good."

---

[1] Dr. Arnold. (See *Life*, by Dean Stanley, p. 617.)

3. For what has been, again and again, the course of human history? Has it not shown a perpetual tendency to deteriorate; a constant danger of creeping paralysis? As long as the stream runs and battles, it is bright and pure; but when it becomes a sluggish marsh, it stagnates into pestilence. "The iris colours its agitation, the frost fixes on its repose." So long as there is continual wrestling of Right against Wrong, shoulder to shoulder, arm to arm, it is well; but when Right has won her partial victory, and Good and Evil lie flat together, in truce and compromise, it ceases to be well. Then habit, custom, convention, commodity, give their bias to the world. The salt loses its savour. The unreplenished lamp burns dim. Truths once vitally true are treated as truisms and despised. Living faiths degenerate into dead theologies. Burning watchwords are degraded into acrid shibboleths. "Virtue is tamed out of her splendid passion." The moral sense is drugged with the opiates of conventionality. Vice decks herself in phylacteries, and

walks in broad beaten paths. Nations bow in the House of Rimmon, and Prophets have no reproof. Words change their meaning. Enthusiasm is dubbed "fanaticism;" lust is called gallantry; the sins of youth are "soft infirmities in the blood;" cheating is but sharp business; dishonest gains are only "the ways of trade." Churches split themselves into parties and are lashed into excitement about paltry trivialities. Good customs, degenerating into mechanical practices, corrupt the world. What was once a mark of religion becomes a badge of party profession. All society becomes rotten to the core. Then amid the mist and the low noises, "far off a solitary trumpet sounds," and lo! God has called forth one, or two, or three of His servants.[1]

[1] "Always it is the individual that works for progress, not the age. It was the age that made away with Socrates by poison; it was the age which burnt Huss at the stake. The ages have always been the same."—GÖTHE.

"Was ist Mehrheit? Mehrheit ist ein Unsinn,
Verstand ist stets bei Wen'gen nur gewesen."

"A mass, that is to say, collective mediocrity."—J. S. MILL, *Liberty*, p. 119.

They through grace obey the calling. He has laid upon their heads the hands of invisible consecration. While they are musing, the fire of God burns within them, and at last they speak with their tongues. Then they devote themselves to some great cause; they fling self-interest to the winds; they tear away the accumulated cobwebs of venerable sophistry; "they smite the hoary head of inveterate abuse." Against the subterfuges of a heartless and self-seeking society they raise the Eternal Standard of the moral law. They confront conventionalism with sincerity. They pay no respect to the external decorum of hypocritical societies. They denounce falsehood, robbery, and wrong. They plead the cause of oppressed humanity. What follows? A roar of execration. They please none. They belong to no party, and therefore all parties hate them. In vain the

"When such a man as thou art is born into the world . . . . where with the soul of an apostle and the courage of a martyr he has singly to push his way among the heartless and aimless crowds that vegetate without living, the atmosphere suffocates him, and he dies. Hated by sinners the mock of fools, disliked

warning sounds to the nations, "Touch not mine Anointed and do my Prophets no harm." In all ages alike the Pharisees, who are rich, deride them; the Sadducees lay cunning traps to catch them; the Herodians regard them as persons politically dangerous. Every merit is denied them; they are fools, they are fanatics, they are Samaritans; they have a devil, and are mad; they are Arians, Socinians, Sabellians, heretics; they are Quixotic, Utopian, unpractical; they have no moderation; they are actuated by a mawkish sentimentality; their learning is ignorance, their aim mischief, their zeal pretence; they "appeal to none but the half-educated"; none of the Scribes or Pharisees

by the envious, abandoned by the weak, what can he do but return to God, weary with having laboured in vain, in sorrow at having accomplished nothing? The world remains in all its vileness and all its hatefulness, and this is what men call the triumph of good sense over enthusiasm."—GEORGE SAND.

Such language is not unnatural on the lips of those who have no real belief in God or in Immortality: but the very object of all Scripture—and most of all the object of our Lord's teaching—was to lead us to look to the eternal fruitfulness of all self-sacrifice in the cause of good, however complete its apparent failure.

believe in them. They might say with St. Gregory of Nazianzus that they have "more stones thrown at them than other men have flowers." Did not Christ say it should be so? If they called the Master of the house Beelzebub, how much more them of His household? Said He not that the blessings which He gave should be "with persecutions"? In soft days like these, when Religion walks in silver slippers, there do seem to be some good men whom all men praise. They cut against the grain of no prejudices; they never run counter to traditional opinions; they are judiciously reticent about current errors; every one speaks well of them; they enjoy a beatitude of benedictions which Christ never promised. And there are many timid, cautious natures — men who spread their sails to every shifting breeze of popularity, and would not speak a bold word against a dominant party, or a dominant prejudice, or a triumphant error— not to save their lives. Well, men differ; peace be with these; let them be happy in their armchairs; let them "make the best of both worlds," and be prosperous candidates for amaranthine crowns. The secret of such success is easy.[1] But this has not been the lot—has never, in this or in any age been the lot of God's noblest Saints. Mention me one among them all—one slayer of monsters, one stormer of abuses, one reformer of Churches, one champion of the wronged—who has not been hated and abused! When God in bad times has good soldiers, He places them in the thick of the battle, and they have fallen under a monument of darts. Near Him, they have been near the fire.[2] For them as for

---

[1] "Mistiness is the mother of wisdom. A man who can set down half-a-dozen general propositions, which escape from destroying one another only by being diluted into truisms, who can hold the balance between opposites so skilfully as to do without fulcrum and beam; who never enunciates a truth without guarding himself against being supposed to exclude the contra dictory—this is your safe man, and the hope of the Church; this is what the Church is said to want . . . sensible, temperate, sober, well-judging men, to guide it through the channel of no-meaning, between the Scylla and Charybdis of Yes and No."—J. H. NEWMAN, *Essays*, i. 301.

[2] Διὸ φησὶν ὁ Σωτήρ, Ὁ ἐγγύς μου ἐγγὺς τοῦ πυρός· ὁ δὲ μακρὰν ἀπ' ἐμοῦ, μακρὸν ἀπὸ τῆς βασιλείας.—DIDYMUS on Ps. lxxxviii. 8.

the old Moslem, "Paradise has been prefigured under the shadow of the crossing scimitars."[1] See how they have sunk to the ground with bleeding feet on the world's highway, whereon often till death they have walked well-nigh alone! But what happens? They have never failed—never ultimately failed; they have startled the deep slumber of false opinions; they have thrilled a pang of noble shame through callous consciences; they become magnetic. Into the next age, if not into their own, "they flash an epidemic of nobleness."

> "They utter but a thought,
> And it becomes a proverb for the state;
> They write a sentence in a studious mood:
> It is a saying for a hemisphere."

Yes, their goal becomes a starting-point of their followers; their heresy the truth of churches; the sons of their murderers build their tombs. But indeed they need no tombs; for their tombs are reared in the gratitude of

---

[1] Compare ἐγγὺς μαχαίρας, ἐγγὺς Θεοῦ· μεταξὺ μαχαίρας, μεταξὺ Θεοῦ.—IGNAT. *ad Smyr.* 4.

nations, and their epitaphs are written on the ruins of the lies which they have annihilated, and the immoral tyrannies which they have overthrown.[1]

4. See if it has not been so. Glance first at the history of the chosen people, which best you know. Israel had gone down into Egypt, and in the torpid civilisation of that sluggish soil—amid the leeks and the melons, the flesh-pots and the cucumbers—they were fast sinking into a nation of sensual slaves. Then in the burning bush God appeared to Moses, and sent

---

[1] In his *Essay on Liberty* (p. 52) Mr. Mill speaks of the dictum that "truth always triumphs over persecution," as "one of those pleasant falsehoods which men repeat after one another till they turn into commonplaces, but which all experience refutes. . . . To speak only of religious opinions: the Reformation broke out at least twenty times before Luther, and was put down. Arnold of Brescia was put down. Fra Dolcino was put down. Savonarola was put down. The Albigenses were put down. The Lollards were put down. The Hussites were put down. Even after the era of Luther wherever persecution was persisted in it was successful." It is undeniable that truths may be suppressed for a time; but surely the testimony borne by all history is that truth, in spite of persecution, does tend in the long run to establish itself and to prevail.

him to rouse this dull people; and with plague, and conflict, and victory, and the rolling waters of the sea, he led them into the free air of the wilderness. And when, even in the wilderness, they relapsed into lust and sloth, and—falling into the accursed trap set for them by Balaam son of Beor — would have been consumed, Phinehas, the son of Eleazar, the son of Aaron the priest, once more saved them,—piercing adulterer and adulteress with one thrust of his avenging spear. Then they conquered Canaan, but, again and again sinking into the same idolatry, the same degradation, they became a prey to all the surrounding tribes. How did God deliver them? By better men than common men; by braver men than cautious men; by men who would not shelter themselves in refuges of lies; by men whose love to Him still burned like a fire on the altar of noble hearts, not yet buried under the whitening embers of immoral acquiescence. Wild times needed wild remedies. From Moab, from Amalek, from Canaan, from the Amorite, from the Philistine, the wooden dagger of Ehud, the flashing torch of Gideon, the burning inspiration of Deborah, the rude sword of Jephthah, the rough strength of Samson, the stainless ephod of Samuel, set them free. What was the one grand quality of all these men? It was Courage. Not mere physical courage—though that is something—but the moral courage which towered behind the physical courage; the faith in right which puts an invincible sword into the grasp of resolution; the courage which so hates and despises wrong-doing, that in facing evil it is not afraid to die. I may be speaking to some young men for whom the day shall come on which they may need the courage to risk life, or things as dear as life, in confronting guilty tyranny, or strong oppression, or conventional falsehood, or immoral custom. Well, let them do it, and not be afraid. Gideon's 300 routed the Amalekites; the 300 at Thermopylæ faced the myriads of Xerxes; the three at the Milvian bridge saved Rome from the hosts of Porsena. Are these but dead facts of history or of legend?

Do they need more modern, and very humble examples? Well then, let me tell them of the old woman whose dauntless bearing in the face of a surging tumult, saved the only two houses that were saved in Queen Square at the Bristol riots; of the single verger who saved the cathedral in that city by resolutely closing and barricading the door in the face of the raging mob; of the single sentinel who, in the lifetime of some here, confronted thousands at the entrance of Downing Street, and prevented them from attacking the house of the Prime Minister, by telling them that except over his body not a man should pass,—and who so woke their admiration that they gave him three cheers and passed on. "Do the thing and scorn the consequence." It was the motto of one of our bravest generals in the Indian mutiny.[1] It was the motto of the judges and heroes of Israel. If we are to do any real good in the world, it must be ours.

[1] Colonel Neill. See Sir J. Kaye's *History of the Indian Mutiny*, ii. 265.

5. But a far rarer, more splendid, more effective thing than the physical courage of warriors was the spiritual and moral courage of the Hebrew Prophets. They had to take their stand, not only against brute violence, but against perverse authority and corrupted religion; against hypocritic priests and godless kings; against the monopolists of orthodoxy and the masters of armies.[1] Well might they shrink from the hard task. One of them was diffident;[2] another was a poor peasant;[3] another was called when a mere boy;[4] and in the bitter wail of Jeremiah,[5] you may hear how painfully they felt the task that was laid upon them. Yet how bravely they performed it! Before the terrible Jezebel and her Baal priesthood Elijah takes his stand;[6] he confronts Ahab at the vineyard gate of his murdered victim;[7] Zechariah rebukes the

---

[1] See Jer. i. 10; v. 31; xviii. 7; xxv. 17, 11; Ezek. xxii. 26, &c.
[2] Is. vi. 5.   [3] Amos vii. 14.   [4] Jer. i. 6.
[5] Jer. xx. 7-18.   [6] 1 Kings. xviii. 15.   [7] 1 Kings xxi. 18.

apostatising Joash;[1] at the high priests Pashur and Amaziah, Jeremiah[2] and Amos[3] hurl their defiant curse; into the palace of Herod, the prophet of the desert strides with his blunt reproof. When religion in Judah had degenerated into gorgeous externalism, the message of the prophets was a protest for everlasting truths. Sequences of colours—shapes of vestments—methods of ablution—repetitions of formulæ—archæological disputes about the interpretation of rubrics—these are not religion; have nothing to do with pure religion and undefiled. "I will have mercy and not sacrifice."[4] "Your new moons and fasts and feasts I cannot away with;"[5] but "wash you, make you clean, put away the evil of your doings from before Mine eyes."[6] Not "thousands of rams, or ten thousands of rivers of oil," but what the Lord requires of thee is "to do justly, and to love mercy, and to walk humbly with thy God."[7]

---

[1] 2 Chr. xxiv. 20.   [2] Jer. xx. 3-6.   [3] Amos vii. 17.
[4] Hos. vi. 6; Matt. ix. 13; xii. 7.   [5] Is. i. 13, 14.
[6] Is. i. 16.   [7] Mic. vi. 6-8.

These were the messages of the prophets, and these the truths which might have saved the chosen people. And though the chosen people, like all people, murdered their prophets and slew those who were sent unto them, these are the truths which have again and again regenerated the world. They are truths which raise their eternal protest against false types of goodness and false types of orthodoxy, and even if destroyed for a time they spring up again. "So do we see a vigorous blade spring out of its seed; the dead and rotten parts fall off on all sides of it; it shoots up; it pushes its way higher; it emerges; it rises to the top; it cuts the upper air, and exults in the light of day."[1]

6. And our blessed Lord came to strengthen, to inspire, to stamp with divinest sanction, to render alone and eternally effectual by His life and by His death—this work and this protest—this hard fighting and this high testimony

---

[1] Morley, *University Sermons*, p. 51.

—of man for men. The tendency of Churches to settle down contentedly into sham orthodoxy and spurious religion has never ceased; and again and again has the Holy Spirit of Christ broken up the fountains of the great deep of individuality to pour its lustral wave over the putrescent world. By the Apostles first,—by the flashing impetuosity of Peter; by the stainless asceticism of James; by the love and the lightning of John; by the heroism and dauntlessness of Paul—He carried on His work. Then, after the Apostles, came the Martyrs. During centuries of active and passive struggle when they could do nothing else, they died. And so "by the unresistible might of weakness," as with the daring of "a host of Scævolas," Justin, Ignatius, Polycarp, Cyprian, Lawrence, Sebastian, Pothinus, Blandina, Felicitas—philosophers, bishops, deacons, soldiers, old men, boys, maidens—they shook the world. And then when other types were needed of courageous protest and courageous individuality, to liberate souls from the confusion of a dying society in the third century, St. Antony fled into the desert; amid the wreck of empire, in the sixth century, St. Benedict founded a noble order of monasticism; in the midst of wealth and corruption, in the thirteenth century, St. Francis of Assisi became the prophet of the poor. When the life of the Church grew more and more corrupt—when the revival of letters had made of Christianity a coarse because a less excusable Paganism—when Pope after Pope was a monster of avarice and crime,[1] the wind of Heaven was still blowing where it listed, and pure foreheads were still mitred with the Pentecostal flame. In dissolute Florence the mighty voice of Savonarola repeated the denunciations of Amos against dissolute Jerusalem. In England the words of Wyclif, in Bohemia the words of Huss, denouncing usurpation, exposing falsehood, proclaiming truth, thrilled into the hearts of the people. In vain the guilty confederacies of priests and rulers

---

[1] I need but mention the names of Paul II., Sixtus IV., Innocent VIII.. Alexander VI., Julius II., and Leo X.

burned Savonarola, burned Huss, exhumed and scattered to the winds the bones of Wyclif. Men may be burned, truth cannot be burnt. Against the mitred atheism and cultured vice of Leo X. arose one poor monk, and shook the worst engines of spiritual tyranny for ever to the ground. Tetzel was impudently selling his pardons and indulgences, and shamelessly demoralising the people with all the power of the Papacy to back him, when Luther sprang into the thick of the battle. He nailed his theses to the cathedral door of Wittenberg; he flung into the flames the papal bull of condemnation; strong in the simple invincibility of an awakened sense of truth and justice, he faced emperors, popes, dukes, cardinals, doctors, theologians.[1] In vain they told him

---

[1] "Nam Deus me invitum et nescium in haec tragica duxit, omnibus amicis mihi dissuadentibus. Sathan saepe mihi dixit, Quid si falsum esset dogma tuum, quod Papam monachos mi sam et tantos cultus confundis?"—*Colloquia*, ii. 12. "Nam Christum praedicare est res ardua et periculosissima. Si ego olim scivissem hujus ministerii difficultatem, nunquam praedicassem."—*Id.* i. 13.

of perils, of imprisonment and assassination; "Were there as many devils in Worms as there are tiles on the roofs, I would go there." "Here stand I; I can no other; God help me." They bid him moderate his words; he will not moderate his words; "the word of God," he says, "is a war, a sword, a perdition, a stumbling-block, a ruin."[1] So he stormed, and so he set free the fettered conscience of mankind. And many rose to continue his work. In Scotland, Knox arose, of whom the Regent Morton said, "Here lies one who never feared the face of man;" who said himself that "he had looked in the faces of many angry men." When he was working in chains on the galleys in France, they brought him an image of the Virgin, and bade him worship the mother of God. "Mother of God," he exclaimed, "it is a pented bredd" (or board), and he flung it into the river to sink or swim. "Who are

[1] It was on the occasion of his being invited by the Elector of Metz to meet the Spanish Ambassador at dinner. "Verbum Dei bellum est, gladius est, perditio est, scandalum est, ruina est."—LUTHER, *Colloquies.*

you," said Mary Queen of Scots to him, "that presume to school the nobles and sovereign of this realm?" "Madam," he answers, "a subject born within the same." "Have you hope?" they ask him on his deathbed, when he can no longer speak ; and lifting his hand he pointed upwards with his finger, and so, pointing to heaven, he died. He died, but not his work; that was being continued when the *Mayflower* sailed from Delft Haven to found on the grand principles of Puritanism the mighty Republic of the West. It was being continued when Hampden and Cromwell were fighting, and Milton uttering words of fire, to save England from the Star Chamber and from ship-money, from the divine right of an unscrupulous tyranny and from the ruthless intolerance of a narrow ecclesiasticism. And when again Protestantism had run to the dregs, when the Church of England—the Church of Cranmer and Latimer—the Church of Jeremy Taylor and Andrewes—the Church of Butler and Tillotson—the Church of Ken and Wilson—had grown sleepy and effete, showing everywhere the trail of nepotism, worldliness, and sloth, smitten with the disease of contented commonplace, once more the fire of God burst forth to scathe the very cedars, while the brambles in their dense undergrowth were being consumed. It broke forth in the last century, in the voices of Wesley and Whitefield, which shamed into repentance and startled into decency, a dissolute and faithless age.[1]

[1] The famous lines of Cowper on Whitefield are at once so beautiful as a poem, so true as a picture, and so powerful as a warning, and they bear so directly on much that I have been saying that I venture to quote them once more:—

"Leuconomus (beneath well-sounding Greek
  I slur a name a poet must not speak)
Stood pilloried on Infamy's high stage,
And bore the pelting scorn of half an age,
The very worst of slander, and the blot
Of every dart that malice ever shot.
The man that mentioned him at once dismissed
All mercy from his lips, and sneered and hissed.
His crimes were such as Sodom never knew,
And Perjury stood up to swear all true;
His aim was mischief, and his zeal pretence,
His speech rebellion against common sense;
A knave, when tried on Honesty's plain rule,
And when by that of Reason a mere fool;

7. What is all this to us? Nothing, if life be nothing; nothing, "if the chief use and market of our time be but to sleep and feed;" nothing, if the main object of life be in the vulgar sense "to get on;" nothing, if to puff and push our way into rank, or to toil and

> The world's best comfort was, his doom was pass'd,
> Die when he might, he must be damned at last.
>   Now, Truth, perform thine office. Waft aside
> The curtain drawn by prejudice and pride,
> Reveal (the man is dead) to wondering eyes
> This more than monster in his native guise.
>   He loved the world that hated him; the tear
> That dropped upon his Bible was sincere.
> Assailed by scandal, and the tongue of strife,
> His only answer was a blameless life,
> And he that forged, and he that threw the dart
> Had each a brother's interest in his heart.
> Paul's love of Christ, and steadiness unbribed
> Were copied close in him, and well transcribed;
>   *   *   *   *
> Like him he laboured, and like him content
> To bear it, suffered shame where'er he went.
>   Blush, Calumny: and write upon his tomb,
> If honest eulogy will leave thee room,
> Thy deep repentance of thy thousand lies,
> Which, aimed at him, have pierced the offended skies,
> And say, Blot out my sin confess'd, deplored,
> Against Thine image in Thy saint, O Lord!"
>   COWPER'S *Hope*.

moil for money, and then to spend it on ourselves, or accumulate it in masses for the aggrandisement of our families be deemed a worthy life; nothing, if we were only born to indulge, like natural brute beasts, our meanest passions; nothing, if the sigh of Jesus were nothing, or if He would find no wrongs to sigh for now. But the millennium surely has not yet begun! Even in this our age good men do find something to do, and something for which to suffer, and be abused. Clarkson and Wilberforce and Zachary Macaulay found that there was the slave-trade to overthrow.[1] Eliot and Martyn and Heber found heathen to convert. Charles Mackenzie and Coleridge Patteson found martyrdoms to face. Simeon and Venn

---

[1] The inscription under the bust of Zachary Macaulay in Westminster Abbey was written by Sir Robert Inglis, and is worth preserving :—" In grateful remembrance of Zachary Macaulay, who, during a protracted life, with an intense but quiet perseverance, which no success could relax, no reverse could subdue, no toil, privations, or reproach could daunt, devoted his time, talents, fortune, and all the energies of his mind and body to the service of the most injured and helpless of mankind."

found an evangelical movement to carry on. Arnold and Cotton found public schools to elevate and purify. Howard and Elizabeth Fry found prisons to regenerate. Raikes and Pounds found Sunday-schools to establish. Pestalozzi and Fröbel found infants to teach. Bell and Lancaster found the system of our national education to establish. Mary Stanley and Florence Nightingale crossed rough seas to nurse dying soldiers. An American citizen, George Peabody, as we heard last Sunday, achieved the astonishing virtue of parting with his money before he was dead. Some have been ears to the deaf; some eyes to the blind; some, fathers and mothers to the orphaned; some, tender nurses to the little ones; some have seen justice done to the little chimney-sweep, and the little factory child, and the little acrobat; some have clutched, are still clutching, by the throat the fiend of intemperance, and all these, thank God, have found followers. A good many have, on the whole, escaped the average; have shaken off from their robes the accumulated dust of immoral acquiescence; have learnt to regard life "not as an adventure, or a pleasure, but as a serious affair—a task assigned to each of us; a duty, to learn which trouble is necessary; a work which must be continued to our last hour." And these have been the great good men "who stretched out their strong arms to bring down Heaven upon our earth."

8. And to all of us the record of the good men who have gone before us, is as a trumpet's blast to make us cry

"O that the forces indeed were arrayed! O joy of the onset!
  Sound, thou trumpet of God; come forth, great cause, to array us!
  King and leader, appear; thy soldiers, sorrowing, call thee!"

But He, the King and Leader, answers, "Walk in My steps, as these did. They tended My sheep; they fed My lambs; they flung the offenders of My innocents with millstones round their necks into the sea; they crushed the viper-head of lies; they quenched the fire of intolerance; they dashed their hands on the lion-mouth of tyranny; they set at liberty the bruised victims of oppression." They did all this: can you do nothing? or is it that you are too much pledged to, and immersed in, the guilty customs and false aims of the world to even try to amend them? How can you speak for tolerance, if you be an anonymous slanderer and savage persecutor of other men's opinions? how for truth, if there be a lie in your right hand? how for freedom, if you be supplying men with the rivets for their chains? how for Christian love, if your whole little nature be acrid with envy and with hate? Or is it that humble duties are too small for you? You could die like a hero; but yet somehow you cannot constrain yourself to do even the smallest good deed in secret self-sacrifice? You feel yourself capable of the most magnanimous martyrdoms, but how can you be expected to give up that favourite falsehood or that mean vice? You want to reform the world; but yet, somehow, you are dishonest in your shop, and mean in your office, and bitter in your language, and impure in your life, and incapable of the most trivial self-denial in the heart of your family! Ah! might not the old Rabbi teach you? "A man who confesses his sin without renouncing it," said Rav Ada bar Matthia, "is like one holding a creeping thing in his hand to whom defilement will continue to cling, though he washes himself with all the water in the world." Ah! do you not feel over your head, all the while, the busy winnowing of Satan's winnow-fan? do you not almost see the mocking smile of the fiend, who knows as well as you how easy it is to be a saint in the sunny dreams of the future, while every step on the dusty road of the present is a step of shame? He is winnowing the mildewed ears of what once might have been wheat in you. While you are so eagerly snatching up vehement opinions in ignorance and passion; while you are trying to crush an enemy by sheer violence, and trample savagely on the fallen; while you are envious; while you are small-minded; while you are swelling the blind clamour against unpopular personages; while you are revelling in false disparagements; while you are holding back, for your own gain, the truths which God has plainly given you to see; while you are living to scrape up money; while you are ready to sacrifice every thing, and every one, to the base gratification of a passion—and, it may be, all the while talking about religion and the world's good—Satan is all the while winnowing you, until "in the dust of your bodies, and the wreck of your souls," nothing shall be left but chaff for him. But *Christ*, too, has *His* awful winnowing-fan, and shall throughly purge His threshing-floor. And oh! where—where in that worthless, mouldering heap of chaff—of lust and envy—of frivolity and vanity—of avarice and intemperance—that niggardly withholding and loveless selfishness—oh, where will be the wheat for His garner? Saints? heroes? reformers of abuses? slayers of monsters? regenerators of the world?—oh, begin first by being decently pure, truthful, kindly, honest, courageous men! Begin by thinking a little of others. Begin by sparing a little of your substance. Begin by giving cups of cold water in Christ's name to Christ's little ones. Begin by doing faithfully the small simple duty which lies nearest you. Begin by trying to feel so much of what Jesus felt when He sighed for a ruined world, as at least not daily to wring with sighs the heart of His ruined children, the heart of His faithful servants. So perchance may He at last send you also, were it but at the eleventh hour, to work in His vineyard. So may He enable you to rise above yourselves and your own selfish interests—to feel what His sigh meant, and to labour in His sick and suffering world.

SERMON IV.

THE WINGS OF A DOVE.

THE WINGS OF A DOVE.

Almighty and everlasting God, who dost govern all things in heaven and earth, mercifully hear the supplications of Thy people, and grant us Thy peace all the days of our life, through Jesus Christ our Lord. Amen.

SERMON IV.

THE WINGS OF A DOVE.

Ps. LV. 6-8.

"*And I said, O that I had wings like a dove, for then would I fly away and be at rest. Lo! then would I get me away far off, and remain in the wilderness. I would make haste to escape because of the stormy wind and tempest.*"[1]

---

[1] It is unnecessary to enter into any critical discussion as to the exact translation of these words. Though not without difficulty, the sense of them seems to be well expressed in the musical and familiar Prayer-book version, from which I have here quoted them. Nor again do I think it necessary to enter into the question whether David is or is not the author of the Psalm. Hitzig attributes it to Jeremiah, and thinks that the faithless friend alluded to is the Priest Pashur, on whom the Prophet denounces so terrible a curse (Jer. xx. 1-6). Ewald again brings it down to the period preceding the Captivity. But the superscription attributes it to David, and not a single valid argument has been adduced to render the authorship improbable.

A GREAT living painter[1] has endeavoured to express the thought of these verses in a beautiful picture. He represents the king seated at eventide upon his palace roof. It was there that he had been sitting on a far different evening,[2] when in pride, fulness of bread, and abundance of idleness,[3] he had opened the wicket gate to that thought of sin which had treacherously betrayed the citadel of his soul to ten thousand terrible enemies, and caused the sun of his glory to set in seas of blood and shame. Very different was his mood on this evening. The crown which he had won from the city of waters was laid aside from the dark hair which had been already silvered by age and sorrow. The arm that smote the giant rests wearily upon the parapet.

The passage in Jeremiah (ix. 2)—"Oh that I had in the wilderness a lodging place for wayfaring men; that I might leave my people to go from them! for they are all adulterers, an assembly of treacherous men"—is an echo of the Psalmist's longing.

[1] Sir F. Leighton.
[2] Sam. xi. 2. "And it came to pass in an eveningtide that David arose from off his bed and walked upon the roof of the king's house."
[3] Ezek. xvi. 49.

What good has all his glory done him? In what respect is he the better for the songs which, setting him above his sovereign, had sung of him that Saul had killed his thousands, and David his ten thousands? Had not his earthly fame trembled into nothingness, like those passing breaths of articulated air? Might he not have been a better and a happier man if God had never taken him away from the sheepfolds, from following the ewes great with young ones? a better and happier man, if, instead of becoming first the captain of outlaws, and then the king of Israel, he had remained the despised of his family, the innocent ruddy shepherd lad, and grown grey with the sun smiting him at noon, and the dews falling on him as he kept watch over his flocks by night? And as these sad thoughts chase each other through his mind, his eye falls on a flock of doves, which seem to be flying far away into the glories of sunset, ere it is swallowed up into the darkening night, and—while a world of hollow friend, and broken system, " made no purple in the distance"—he envies the swift wings which carry to some safe shelter their defenceless innocence. And then, seizing his harp, he pours forth a wail of passionate complaint, and exclaims, "Oh that I had wings like a dove, for then would I fly away and be at rest! I would make haste to escape from the stormy wind and tempest."

How often has the same wish been sighed forth by multitudes of hearts! We are all the more familiar with it, and with the feeling which it expresses, because we have heard it sung so often to that music of Mendelssohn's which seems to shadow forth more than the tongue can utter,—the music so full of tender and infinite yearning, in which we seem to share the hovering of the dove, and to see it scatter the sunlight and the dew from its pure wings as they beat in the air of upper heaven.

> "Oh had I the wings, the wings of a dove,
> Far away, far away would I rove;
> In the wilderness make me a nest,
> And remain there for ever at rest!"

My friends, we have been turning our thoughts lately to the sigh of Jesus. We have seen that it sprang from no transient emotion; that it was not the mere luxury of a sluggish selfishness; but that it was wrung for a moment from the depths of an eternal compassion, and was at once human and divine,—human in its sadness, divine in the energy and toil of self-sacrifice which it inspired. And we have seen that we ought to share in the feelings which caused that sigh, and in the work to which it led; and we have seen something too of the conditions under which we can alone take part in this amelioration of the world. To-day let us, by way of contrast, think a little of this sigh of David, which is the sigh of many men; sighs natural indeed, and excusable indeed, and like the sigh of Jesus so far as they are innocently human, but which have in them, alas, too little of the divine.

How many a man at death, how many a man long before death came, has heaved such sighs! Turn to your Bible, which reflects the varying moods of so many minds, and you will find there the record of a multitude of these sighs of weariness, of discouragement, of self-disgust, of pain. Most ignoble are they when they are prompted by a wretched peevishness like that of Jonah, wishing himself dead because his gourd is withered and because God has spared Nineveh, and so God's mercy has triumphed over his paltry personal credit;[1]—or by a cynical

---

[1] Jon. iv. 8, 9. How deeply instructive is Jonah's sullen wrath because God has not fulfilled the threatened doom upon Nineveh! The temper of the prophet in the Old Testament closely resembles that of the elder brother of the prodigal in the New. "I pray thee, O Lord, was not this my saying when I was yet in my country? Therefore I fled before unto Tarshish: for I knew that Thou art a gracious God and merciful, slow to anger and of great kindness, and repentest Thee of the evil. *Therefore* now, O Lord, take, I beseech thee, my life from me; for it is better for me to die than to live!"—Jon. iv. 2. Jonah might well "know" that "the Eternal is the Eternal, merciful and gracious, long-suffering, and abundant in goodness and truth," because God had proclaimed it to Moses long before (Ex. xxxiv. 6, 7). But it would go hard with men—and not least with many of the best and noblest men who ever lived—if man, not God, were the judge: hardest, perhaps, of all if those men were the judges who profess most loudly a zeal for God's honour. What chance had "publicans and sinners"—nay, what chance of escape had even the King of Saints—when there were Scribes and Pharisees in the judgment seat?

pessimism, like that of the sated Solomon, which, until he is brought to a better mood, sees nothing in life but a universal emptiness;[1] —or by a black suicidal despair like that of Judas Iscariot, aching under the terrible glare of illumination flung upon conscience by accomplished crime. But even the nobler spirits sometimes succumb for a moment to these merely selfish weaknesses. God's greatest saints have sighed not only with the pure pity of Jesus, but with the impatience and short-sightedness of sinful man.

Let us take some instances. Moses had as brave and mighty a heart as ever beat in any breast, yet he exclaims, "Wherefore hast Thou afflicted Thy servant? Have *I* conceived all this people? have I begotten them, that Thou shouldst say unto *me*, Carry them in thy bosom? I am not able to bear all this people alone. If Thou deal thus with me, kill me I pray Thee out of hand, and let me not see my wretchedness."[2] What a sigh is there!

[1] Eccles. i.—ix.   [2] Num. xi. 11—15.

Gideon was a man full of faith, yet he cried, "O my Lord, if the Lord be with us, why then is all this befallen us? But now the Lord hath forsaken us, and delivered us into the hands of the Midianites."[1] What a sigh is there!

There never breathed a more dauntless prophet than Elijah, yet he sat under a juniper tree in the wilderness, and requested for himself that he might die; and said, "It is enough now, O Lord, take away my life; for I am not better than my fathers."[2] How deep a sigh is there! And Job was patient, yet under the pitiless storm of sickness and suffering even Job broke down and cursed the day of his birth.[3] And Jeremiah had schooled into bravery his natural diffidence, yet when Pashur smote him and put him in the stocks, he too burst into the wild cry, "Wherefore came I forth out of the womb to see labour and sorrow, that my day, should be consumed with shame?"[4] And do we not seem to hear the sigh of even the mighty

---

[1] Judg. vi. 13.   [2] 1 Kings xix. 4.
[3] Job iii. 1.   [4] Jer. xx. 14-18.

Baptist, from his cell in the black dungeon of Makor, when he sent to ask Jesus,—then in the gladness of His Galilean spring,—"Art thou He that should come, or do we look for another?"[1] Nay, even Paul, though nothing can wring such sighs from that indomitable soul, is yet in a strait betwixt two, and knows that "to depart and to be with Christ is very far better."[2]

Here then you have the weariness and discouragement of the noblest of mankind. It is not generally because of personal suffering, but either because the world is evil—"Mine eyes burst out with water because men keep not Thy law":[3]—or because life is full of trials, "Few and evil have the days of the years of my life been, and have not attained unto the days of the years of the life of my fathers in the days of their pilgrimage":[4]—or because work is very dreary, and seems to fail, "Since I came to Pharaoh to speak in

---

[1] Matt. xi. 3.
[2] Phil. i. 23. πολλῷ μᾶλλον κρεῖσσον.
[3] Ps. cxix. 136; Jer. xiii. 17; Phil. iii. 18.
[4] Gen. xlvii. 9; Ps. xxxix. 12.

Thy name, he hath done evil to Thy people; neither hast Thou delivered Thy people at all."[1] Yes, all good men have had to fight with impenetrable stupidity, and hard Pharisaism, and dominant wickedness, and religious and irreligious self-conceit. And so the whole Bible is full of sighs. And what are they, in good men (for of the devil's martyrs I shall to-day take no account), but different forms of that agony of the Cross, which, on the awful brink of a lonely death, bearing the mysterious burden of the sins of the whole world, broke forth into that momentary wail of utter agony, *Eli, Eli, lama sabachthani*— "My God, my God, why hast Thou forsaken me?"

Now, my brethren, one of the elements in Scripture which makes it so inestimably valuable, is that it is so essentially human, and so profoundly true to nature; so inartificial, so simple, sensuous, passionate, as all true history and all true poetry should be. These kings, heroes,

[1] Ex. v. 23.

prophets were just such men as ourselves; their hearts beating like our hearts; their joys and sorrows, their hopes and fears, even such as ours. This same sense of weariness, and discouragement, and willingness to die, we find in secular history: we find it in literature; we find it in our own souls. It is a part of our life. We get tired. We are tired of the daily sameness of life. The rivers run into the sea, yet the sea is not full.[1] The eyes of man are never satisfied. We are tired of the hungry grave, crying like the daughters of the horseleech, "Give, give";[2] tired of the unrelenting past; of the dreary present; of the uncertain future. We are tired of the weary struggle in our own hearts; the to-and-fro conflicting waves of impulse and repression;[3] the broad rejoicing tides of spiritual emotion, and the flat oozy shores of ebbing enthusiasm. Who would not cry with the poor old Scotchwoman, "O it's a sair sight," as he stands in the wynds of Glasgow, or the cellars of Liverpool, or the slums of London? Yes, it's "a sair sight," this

[1] Eccl. i. 7.   [2] Prov. xxx. 15.   [3] Rom. vii. 14-25.

scum and sand in the impure fringe of the glittering wave of civilisation. The old historian said that no man had ever lived without coming to a day in his life when he cared nothing if he were to see no morrow. Again and again we feel inclined to cry with the sad thinker, at the end of another self-reproaching year, " Eternity, be thou my refuge!"[1] Men whose lives have been devoted to pleasure feel it.

> " Through life's drear road, so dim and dirty,
> I have dragged on to three-and-thirty;
> What have those years brought to me?
> Nothing except thirty-three;"

so wrote Lord Byron.

A godless experience curdles at once into acrid pessimism. It is the philosophy at this moment of many materialists,—the sour unwholesome sediment left in souls from which all hope has evaporated. It is Schopenhauer, saying that our condition is so utterly wretched, that total annihilation would be preferable;

---

[1] "*Éternité, deviens mon asile!*" These words were inscribed by his own request on the tomb of Senancour.

that the existence of the world is a matter of grief, and a fundamental misfortune. Such words are the defiant curse of deliberate unbelief; but if this life were everything, many would say the same. We find this hopelessness and dissatisfaction in every rank. Now it is Diocletian declaring that planting cabbages at Salona is better than ruling the world in Byzantium.[1] Now it is Severus saying he has been everything, from a common peasant to a victorious emperor, and nothing is of any good.[2] Now it is Abderrahman the Magnificent, recording that in his life he has had but fourteen happy days.[3] Now it is St. Augustine saying, "Let a man consider the sources of his happiness, and if it will abide with him alway: if not it is of the streams of Babylon, let him sit down by it and weep." Now it is St. Bernard saying of human life that its beginning is blindness, its continuance toil, its sum-total emptiness, "*Initium caecitas, progressio labor, omnia vanitas.*

[1] Gibbon (ed. Milman), i. 399.
[2] "*Omnia fui et nihil expedit.*"—*Hist. Aug.*
[3] Gibbon, v. 196.

Now it is Petrarch saying, "I see not what anything in the world can give me save tears." Now it is Richard Hooker saying, "I have lived to see that the world is made up of perturbations, and have been long preparing to leave it." Now it is Luther saying, "I am weary of life if this can be called life. There is nothing which would give me pleasure; I am utterly weary. I pray that the Lord will come forthwith, and carry me home." Now it is Whitefield saying, "Lord, I am weary not of Thy work, but in Thy work. Let me speak for Thee once more, then seal Thy truth and die." So then History, the life-histories of men, are full of these sad sighs.

And so too is literature. We hear the sigh in Shakespeare's famous sonnet,

> "Tired with all these, for restful death I cry."

It is Cowper's,

> "O for a lodge in some vast wilderness,
> Some boundless contiguity of shade,
> Where rumour of oppression and deceit,
> Of unsuccessful and successful war,
> Might never reach me more."

It is Shelley's,

> "I could lie down like a tired child,
> And weep away this life of care."

"Sir, are you truly conscious of the greatness of God?" said a forward, uninvited clergyman who thrust himself by the bedside of Montesquieu when his own clergyman had left him. "Yes," said the dying philosopher, "and of the littleness of man," and so he died. And what a sigh was there!

In yonder transept lie buried the mortal bodies of two great moralists. They knew the world well; they had seen life in all its phases; they were eminently successful; they gained large wealth; they were universally honoured. One would have said that to these two, to Charles Dickens and William Thackeray, life had given some of its best gifts. What was their experience? "Life," said Dickens, "seems to me the saddest dream that was ever dreamed." "*Vanitas vanitatum*," such are the words with which Thackeray ended his most famous work of fiction; "which of us is happy in this world?

which of us has what he desires, or having it is satisfied?"

All these, and hundreds more, are sighs wrung from that inexorable weariness, which, as the great Bossuet said, lies at the bases of our life. None have better expressed it, and expressed at the same time the thoughts which should be the remedy for all that is not permissible in the permanent indulgence of such emotions, than that brave and good man who was, for a time too brief for us, and too brief for the world, a Canon of this Abbey,—Charles Kingsley. He sings how once, on the merry Christmas-eve, he went sighing over the moorland—

"O never sin, and want, and woe, this earth will leave,
 And the bells but mock the wailing round they ring so cheery,
 How long, O Lord, before Thou come again?"—

And how such despairing thoughts were rebuked by the joyous clamour of the wild fowl on the mere, reminding him of God. And again, in the sweet verses—

" Wild, wild wind, wilt thou never cease thy sighing,
   Dark, dark night, wilt thou never wear away?
Cold, cold church, in thy death-sleep lying,
   Thy Lent is past, thy Passion here, but not thine Easter Day."

" Peace, faint heart, tho' the night be dark and sighing;
   Rest, fair corpse, where thy Lord Himself hath lain;
Weep, dear Lord, above Thy bride low lying,
   Thy tears shall wake her frozen limbs to life and health again."

The Arab proverb says, my friends, that the remembrance of youth is a sigh; might we not almost say that the epitome and epitaph of all human life, but for the faith in something beyond it, would be a sigh? To-day, this day of the massacre of the Holy Innocents, is the anniversary of the founding, 814 years ago, of this mighty Minster (oh! that we may always love and cherish it!) by Edward the Confessor. Rich with the accumulated records of eight centuries of English life, is it not, for all who know rightly how to read its lessons, an unmistakable memorial of the sum-total of human experience? Look up at these vaulted roofs, hung so high over our heads, and see, how there, and in the gloom of the great aisles, these twinkling lights seem to be swallowed up and lost in mysterious gloom. Such too is human life. And yet—

> "They dreamt not of a perishable home
> Who thus could build."

And the very shadows seem to tell us of the faith of our fathers, that though "clouds and darkness are round about Him, yet righteousness and judgment are the habitation of His seat." And while the Abbey thus prophesies to us of a hope for all who will embrace it beyond the grave, how do its records seem to sum up the sadness and the evanescence of every aim on the hither side of it! Great men, and rich men, and successful men, and princes and warriors lie buried here. Why, the whole book of Ecclesiastes seems to be written on these walls and on these graves![1] To the sensual, to the selfish, to the bitter Pharisee, to the moilers for gold, they say, "Soon, soon thy soul—that soul which thou

---

[1] See the beautiful lecture by the late Canon Kingsley on Westminster Abbey, among his American lectures.

art suffering to be blighted with the ignorance of loveless self-sufficiency, to be eaten away with the leprosy of pleasureless iniquity—soon, soon shall it be required of thee." To the wiser and nobler they say, "Not here! no rest here! no peace! no satisfaction, save such as righteousness and faith can give." Look round you, my friends; many of you in that north transept are sitting on graves which, more thickly than any other spot in the world, hold the relics of England's greatest dead. Beneath your feet lie the mortal bodies of Chatham, of Pitt, of Fox, of Canning, of Castlereagh, of Grattan, of Wilberforce, of Palmerston. Do you think that they never longed for the wings of a dove, to flee away and be at rest? Chatham, with his brain so often clouded, his body so often tortured by disease; Pitt, dying of a heart broken with sorrows and anxieties; Castlereagh, perishing by his own hand, and buried amid shouts of execration, which not even death could extinguish; Canning, sinking to the grave amid the shafts of an envenomed personality? And if these were often discouraged and weary, would not the shades of the poets sigh back to them in antiphon from yonder southern transept? Chaucer, weeping too late for the wanton writings of his youth; Spenser, bewailing the sickness of hope deferred; Butler, whose monument was given lest he who in life wanted bread, in death should lack a stone; Milton

> "On evil days though fallen, and evil tongues;
> In darkness, and with dangers compassed round,
> And solitude."

And if the poets and the statesmen should say to the troubled kings and unhappy queens of yonder royal tombs, "Are ye too become weak as we, are ye become like unto us?" would *they* not answer, "Think not that we were exempted from the common lot of sorrow and disappointment"? Would not Edward the Third so answer, "mighty victor, mighty lord," from his plundered and deserted deathbed? And Richard the Second from the murderous gloom of Pomfret Castle? And the Queen of Scots from her scaffold at

Fotheringay? And Elizabeth with her worn and broken heart? Ah, does not this Abbey, with its 800 years of varied history, confirm the truth which we learn from Scripture, that the air of human life is tremulous with sighs?

6. Well, my brethren, it always seems to me worth while to recognise facts; to bring them out into the full light of consciousness, to look them in the face. And this being the fact respecting human life which we have to face, where is the remedy? what are we to do?

The great resource in every perplexity is to look to Christ. If we look to our Great Example we shall see that He too, even He was forced to sigh for the sad world of sin and death; but notice that the sigh had scarcely been uttered when once more He was engaged in works of mercy and thoughtful care. To sigh is sometimes natural; but to waste time in sighing, to suffer ourselves to be wholly absorbed in the dark side of life, to exclude ourselves from its many and simple gladnesses, is unthankful and useless. However hard the struggle against intolerance, and bigotry, against stupidity and malice, against robbery and wrong, no good and brave life will ever suffer itself to be crippled by conquerable melancholy. If we sigh for our own weaknesses and sins, we cannot indeed fly from ourselves, but we can by the grace of God amend ourselves. If we sigh for our surroundings, no wings of a dove indeed, can take us from these dwellings of Meshech, these tents of Kedar, but by God's grace we may help to make them better and happier places. For, after all, at all times of our pilgrimage—

> "The primal duties shine aloft like stars,
> And charities that soothe, and heal, and bless,
> Lie scattered at the feet of man like flowers."

The lessons of Scripture, the lessons of the life of Christ, the lessons of this Abbey, alike teach us to labour and to wait; they combine to tell us that to every one of us alike, for sorrow and disaster, for weariness and discouragement, God has given us four great and perfect remedies. On these let me say a very few last words.

i. One remedy is *Action:* God taught it to

Moses, "Wherefore criest thou unto me? speak to the children of Israel that they go forward."[1] While there is anything to be done the time given to inactive sorrow is worse than wasted. Sorrow may take from life its delights; but thank God it can never take its duties. At the lowest ebb of dejection we still have much to do; and "that man is very strong and powerful, who has no more hope for himself; who looks not to be loved any more; to be admired any more; to have any more honour or dignity; and who cares not for gratitude; but whose sole thoughts is for others, and who only lives for them."[2] The wings of a dove?—nay, my brethren, let us rather long for the wings of an eagle to fly in the path of God's commandments; let us, with the ancient Rabbi, pray that we may be bold as a leopard, swift as an eagle, bounding as

---

[1] Ex. xiv. 15. "'My beloved are sinking in the sea, and *thou* art making long prayers,' said the Holy One—blessed be He—to Moses. Moses asked, 'What then shall I do?' The Lord said unto Moses, 'Speak unto the children of Israel, that they go forward.'"—*Sotah*, f. 37, c.

[2] Sir A. Helps, *Realmah*.

a stag, brave as a lion, to do the will of our Father in heaven.[1] "Let me work on," said Mendelssohn; "for me too the hour of rest will come." "Doe the next thynge,"—what a grand motto that was! And that was a good motto, *Repos ailleurs.* Work here, rest is elsewhere; wipe thy tears; cease thy sighing; do thy work. "The day is short; the work abundant; the labourers are remiss; the reward is great; the Master presses."[2]

ii. And the remedy is *Patience.* God is patient. "*Patiens quia aeternus.*" His great ones are slandered every day by earth's little, and His wise men judged by fools, and "He makes no ado." His name is blasphemed, His character often hideously misrepresented by those who profess to teach in His name. He bears it all, He has borne with man's falsehood, and littleness, and disobedience, for no one knows how many thousand years. Cannot we too wait? If we do well and suffer for it, can we not take it patiently?[3] "Patient continuance in well

---

[1] *Pesachim,* f. 113, 3.   [2] *Pirke Abhoth.* ii.
[3] 1 Pet. ii. 20

doing," there is a grand remedy for idle tears.[1] "O rest in the Lord and abide patiently upon Him; for they that patiently abide the Lord, those shall inherit the land."[2]

And the remedy is *Faith*. Jesus as He sighed looked up towards heaven. "Two things alone can finally cure the malady of occasional depression—they are God and death."[3] Faith looks up hopefully to God; Hope looks forward fearlessly to death. Is our sigh for our own work? "O cast thy burden on the Lord, and He shall sustain thee."[4] Is our sigh for the world? We did not make the world, and He who made it will guide. One day, when St. Francis was laying before God his troubles and disquietudes, the answer came to him, "Why dost thou trouble thyself, poor little man? I who made thee the shepherd of my order,

---

[1] Rom. ii. 7.

[2] Ps. xxxvii. 7. Patient duty and "waiting upon God" are again and again inculcated in Scripture. See Ps. lxii. 1; Prov. xx. 22; Is. xxx. 15; Gal. vi. 9; Heb. x. 36, &c.

[3] Lacordaire.

[4] Ps. lv. 22.

knowest thou not that I am its supreme protector? If those whom I have called succumb, I will put others in their place, and if none existed I would cause them to be born." "I cannot mend the world," said Luther; "if I thought that I could, I should be the veriest ass alive. Thou must do it, oh my God."

Action, Patience, Faith; lastly, the remedy is *Hope*. "It is good that a man should both hope and quietly wait for the salvation of the Lord."[1] "The worst of evils," says the French proverb, "are those that never come."[2] Things are rarely as bad as they look to us. Elijah cries, "I, even I only am left;"[3] and God tells him that He has 7,000, who have not bowed the knee to Baal. The young man is terror-stricken in besieged Dothan, and Elisha shows him the whole mountain full of the protecting chariots of fire.[4] If we be true and faithful, then rightly

---

[1] Lam. iii. 26.
[2] *Les malheurs des malheurs sont ceux qui n'arrivent jamais.*
[3] 1 Kings xix. 10.
[4] 2 Kings vi. 17. Comp. 2 Chr. xxxii. 7; Ps. lv. 18; xxxiv. 7; lxviii. 17; Matt. xxvi. 53.

considered, our very trials and sorrows are the proofs and pledges to us of a better world beyond, and of a time when God shall finish His own work. Shall the great housekeeper of the world fodder His cattle and water His flowers, and prune his plants and not feed His children?[1]

> " Man's grief is but his grandeur in disguise,
> And discontent is immortality."[2]

7. And surely for those who believe in their Saviour at all, this season tells of Hope. We have been bending in imagination over the Saviour's cradle, we have been listening to the angel songs. Do those songs seem to mock us with false hopes, since God's glory is not manifested fully, and there is little peace on earth? Ah, my brethren, *this* hope at least was not frustrated—that to us was born a Saviour, which is Christ the Lord. He conquered death, and because He broke its dominion, it can have no dominion over us. One day, not far hence, we too shall have the wings of a dove. Though we

[1] Trapp, *New Test.*   [2] Young.

have lien among earth's shards, yet at death, if we be God's children, shall we be as the wings of a dove, which is covered with silver wings, and her feathers like gold.[1] And meanwhile, till that day comes, if we cannot have the wings of a dove, we can have in our very hearts the spirit of Christ, which is a dovelike spirit.[2] That dove cannot fly in unclean places; it cannot rest upon unholy brows; but if we cleanse our hearts, it will find a shelter with us, and brood tenderly over the storms of life. We are told that while yet the waters of the deluge weighed upon the drowning world, the dove flew back to the ark "and lo! in her mouth an olive leaf plucked off!"[3] The olive leaf is bitter, but it is a sign of peace, and the Jewish legend tells that "the dove said before the Holy One, blessed be He! 'Lord of the Universe! let my food be bitter as an olive, delivered by Thy hands, rather than sweet as honey delivered by the hands of flesh

---

[1] Psalm lxviii. 13.
[2] *Spiritus Jesu, spiritus columbinus.*—Bacon.
[3] Gen. viii. 11.

and blood.'"[1] My friends, however much the deluge may welter round us, that Holy Heavenly Dove of Peace—

> "Sweet dove, the softest, steadiest plume,
> In all the sunbright sky;
> Brightening in ever changeful bloom,
> As breezes change on high,"—

is ready to descend into our hearts and rest therein. And if the plucked leaf, which she bears to us from God in heaven, seem bitter to us, yet none the less is it a leaf of the Tree of Life,—a green leaf from that tree "whose leaves are for the healing of the nations."

[1] *Sanhedrin*, f. 108, 2. (Comp. Prov. xxx. 8, *Heb.*)

SERMON V.

WORK IN THE GROANING CREATION.

WORK IN THE GROANING CREATION.

"Who the Creator loves, created might
Dreads not."—COLERIDGE, *Religious Musings*.

"Infelix homo qui scit illa omnia, Te autem nescit; beatus autem qui Te scit etiamsi illa nesciat. Qui vero et Te et illa novit, non propter illa beatior, sed propter Te solum beatus est si cognoscens Te, sicut Deum glorificet et gratias agat, et non evanescat in cogitationibus suis."—AUG. *Conf.* v. 4.

"We live in a world which is full of misery and ignorance, and the plain duty of each and all of us is to try and make the little corner he can influence somewhat less miserable and somewhat less ignorant than it was before he entered it."—HUXLEY, *Lay Sermons*, p. 159.

O Almighty and most merciful God, of Thy bountiful goodness keep us, we beseech Thee, from all things that may hurt us, that we being ready, both in body and mind, may cheerfully accomplish those things that Thou wouldest have done, through Jesus Christ our Lord. Amen.

SERMON V.

WORK IN THE GROANING CREATION.

GEN. I. 31.

"And God saw everything that He had made, and behold it was very good."

ROM. VIII. 22.

"For we know that the whole creation groaneth and travaileth in pain together until now." [1]

REV. XXII. 3.

"And there shall be no more curse."

1. IN those three texts, my brethren, you have the past, the present, the future of our earth;

---

[1] The Greek of the verse is οἴδαμεν γὰρ ὅτι πᾶσα ἡ κτίσις συστενάζει ἄχρι τοῦ νῦν. It seems to me that the English version is right in rendering κτίσις here by "creation." The same word is used indeed in Mark xvi. 15 and Col. i. 23, where it is rendered "to every creature," because in these passages the reference is mainly to mankind; and some have argued that in this passage

what was, what is, what shall be; the perfectness which man has marred, the punishment which he is enduring, the hope to which he looks. What share we may have in the marring or the mending of this our transitory dwelling, that is our main subject to-day.

We have been considering on previous Sundays the sigh of Jesus over a disordered and suffering world. We saw that it was a sigh wrung from the spirit of eternal compassion, and yet that not for one moment did it stay the course of holy beneficence. We saw further that every good man must feel for the miseries which caused that sigh; that by our love to God and to His Christ we are bound to share in the work which

<hr />

the attribution to inanimate nature, or to the unintelligent creation of earnest "expectation" (*apokaradokia*, "looking eagerly with outstretched head"), and intense absorption in sorrowful yearning, would be too strong and poetical. It differs, however, but little from the Scripture language (Ps. xcviii. 7 ; Is. xxxv. 1 ; Hos. ii. 21, &c.) with which St. Paul had been familiar from his childhood, and must be taken to express the longings of nature in its present disordered condition (in which, as an old divine says, it represents, not a *stasis* but an *apostasis*), for the manifestation of a glory and liberty which have been promised, but which are still in the future (2 Pet. iii. 10-13).

may alleviate those miseries; that the chief cause of them all is sin; that therefore the first and best conditions of true work for Christ are personal innocence and personal holiness; that they who, in one form or other, have devoted their lives to this great work of amelioration have been amongst the noblest of mankind. We saw further that they who share Christ's work must also share His sorrow, but that for the deep weariness and discouragement which besets all life, even in the midst of such efforts as these, the divinely appointed remedies are Action and Patience, Faith and Hope. Surely, my friends, if we have tried to grasp these thoughts, they are not questionable, not ignoble thoughts, but such as may inspire our own lives, and irradiate with a glow of brighter happiness the lives of those around us. Is it not an inspiring and cheering thought to regard our life as a term of service in the high cause of God, and ourselves as "co-operant units" in His vast designs? It is not, of course, possible in a few sermons to deal systematically with the whole of this great subject, nor is it necessary to work out all its details. The details are best left to the individual conscience, which will direct us how to turn to best profit in God's service the separate gifts of each of us. But surely *the ideal* is a high and holy one, nor could we, I think, either as citizens or as Christians, have better ended the old year and begun the new, than by considering thus seriously the example of our Lord, and by asking the aid of His Holy Spirit that we may walk in His steps, bearing humbly and manfully whatever cross He may see fit to send us. Not to despair of good either for ourselves or for the world; not to acquiesce in evil, whether the world's evil or our own, these alone are grand lessons. For the truest men are they in whose bosom there burns an inextinguishable hope. The day may set for them into starless night, but still on the dark horizon,

> "Hope, a soaring eagle, burns
> Above the unrisen morrow."

Is not this a part at least of St. Paul's meaning when he says that " We are saved by hope"?[1] What was the very heart and essence of the religion of Israel for 2,000 years—let me say rather of the religion of humanity itself for still more millenniums—but a fixed Messianic hope? Satan has defeated us. He has lost us Paradise. Yet, even at the moment of the lost Paradise, the hope was granted that we should one day crush the serpent's head. We have plucked the bitter fruit of the Tree of the knowledge of evil, yet the

---

[1] Rom. viii. 24. τῇ γὰρ ἐλπίδι ἐσώθημεν, literally "For by (or *in*) hope" (the article here seems to be generic) "we were saved." It is true that Faith not Hope is always put forward in Scripture as the receptive instrument by which we are saved, but hope, as Tholuck says, may here be regarded as "faith in its prospective attitude." By hope we appropriate to ourselves and enjoy—to the great support and blessing of our life—the promised salvation which we embraced through faith (comp. Col. i. 23). Again, in another passage, Luke vii. 47, Love seems to be represented as the main element in being forgiven, so that all the three great Christian Virtues appear to co-operate as instrumental causes in our enjoyment of the benefits won for us by the Atoning work of Christ. There can be no true faith without hope; and faith works by love. Spiritual conditions do not admit of the clear sequence of earthly events. The past tense—"we were saved"—is used because it refers backwards to the time of conversion.

M

Tree of Life still stands in the garden of God, and it was a legend of deep meaning which told that a seed of that tree was brought to Adam, and that from it sprang that other Tree of Life from which the Cross was made. And, again, what is the religion of all Christians but a fixed Messianic hope? The Cross is the sign of eternal conquest. Is it the sign of conquest for ourselves only? dare we so confine its significance? Is its divine power to be dwarfed into the narrowness of self-congratulation, or into the slightly expanded egotism which shall see nothing more in Christ's work than the salvation of some handful of a Church, or some fraction of a sect? Are we to eternise and deify

> " The sin of self, who in the universe,
>   As in a mirror sees her fond face shown,
>   And crying 'I' would have the world say 'I,'
>   And all things perish so but she endure"?

Not so! Christ who has left us is still with us; and He shall return again. And when He returns, He shall bruise Satan under our feet;

He shall restore all things, He shall subdue even the last enemy, Death; to multitudes which no man can number, gathered from east and west, and north and south, He shall bring joy and gladness, and sorrow and sighing shall flee away.[1]

2. We have seen already some glimpses at least of the truth that actively by sympathy, by thoughtfulness, by charity, by unselfishness, by loving one another;—that even passively by abstaining from the fashionable and universal vice of biting and devouring one another;—we have seen that by honesty, by self-reverence, by reverence for others, by obeying the golden rule of "doing unto others as we would they should do unto us," we may do very much to limit the realm of sorrow, and to substitute a golden for an iron sceptre in its sway over human hearts. We have seen, too, that our own inevitable trials and humiliations,—all the neglect, all the insult, all the weariness, all the

[1] Is. xxxv. 10; xxv. 8; Hos. xiii. 14; Heb. ii. 8, 14 15; 1 Cor. xv. 24-28, &c.

disappointment, all the ingratitude, which may befall us,—can be better borne if we be cheerful and active in doing good. Labour for God is the best cure for sorrow, and the best occupation of life, even as the old poet so sweetly sings, if we put a wider and a spiritual meaning into his words,

> "Canst drink the waters of the crispèd spring?
>   O sweet content!
> Swim'st thou in wealth, yet sink'st in thine own tears?
>   O punishment!
> Then he that patiently want's burden bears
> No burden bears, but is a king, a king!
> O sweet content! O sweet, O sweet content!
>   Work apace, apace, apace;
>   Honest labour bears a lovely face."

Something of these truths we have, I hope, seen. But can we to-day push the inquiry yet further, and learn whether it is in our power in any way to mend the flaw which runs for us through the material world; or in any way to diminish for ourselves and for mankind the pressure of that vast weight of laws which exercises over us, undoubtedly, a sway of awful potency? The whole creation groaneth and travaileth in pain together until now; can we—not by any strength of ours, but because God permits and desires it, can we do anything to hasten that blessed hour for which we wait—the hour of the new creation; of the adoption, to wit, the redemption of our body; of the restitution of all things; of the *Palingenesia* of the world?[1]

I think we can. I know that the supposed helplessness of man is a favourite topic of modern materialism, which makes of man the irresponsible tool of forces which he cannot resist, the sport and prey of dumb powers which are alike inexorable and passionless. This philosophy—if we may call it a philosophy—laughs to scorn the notion of a miracle, and makes virtue and vice not the conscious choice of free beings, but the inevitable result of material causes and hereditary impulses, of which in all but semblance, we are the mere automata and slaves. My brethren, into all these

---

[1] Rom. vii. 23; Acts iii. 21; Matt. xix. 28; 2 Thess. iii. 13. &c.

speculations of a baseless atheism, I need not enter. To us, nature means nothing but the sum-total of phenomena which God has created; and since in the idea of nature is included the idea of God, a miracle becomes as natural and as easily conceivable as the most ordinary occurrence.[1] And we *know* that we are free, that God does not mock us, that we can abhor that which is evil, and cleave to that which is good. The laws of nature are nothing, then, for us but observed sequences, and we do not admit that there is anything fearful in their uniformity. It is true that nature drives her ploughshare straight onwards, and heeds not what may be lying in the furrow; it is true that therefore she shows

---

[1] "The soul of man was not produced by heaven and earth, but was breathed immediately from God; so that the ways and proceedings of God with spirits are not included in nature, that is in the laws of heaven and earth, but are reserved to the law of His secret will and grace."—Lord Bacon, *A Confession of Faith.*

"The law of the divine nature enables it to suspend all physical laws, but the existence of a God assumed, the law of the divine nature is as much a law of nature as the laws which it suspends."—Mozley on Miracles, p. 162.

an apparent indifference to human agony; it is true that if the fairest and sweetest child which earth ever saw be left at play in the face of the advancing tide, the tide will still advance and drown the little life; it is true that the fire in its ruthless vividness will roll over the loveliest maiden whose rich dress should catch its flame.[1] Only think of that accident which appalled us six days ago.[2] It is a law that resistance must be equal to force, and that if there be a certain amount of pressure and of vibration, whatever comes of it, a structure will give way, even though, alas, it hurl nearly a hundred human beings, with one flash of horror, into the gulf of death. But is this any reason for a fierce

---

[1] " Près du foyer Constance s'admirait.
    Dieu ! sur sa robe il vole une étincelle !
  Au feu, courez; quand l'esprit l'enivrait
    Tout perdre ainsi ! Quoi ! Mourir—et si belle !
  L'horrible feu ronge avec volupté
    Ses bras, son sein, et l'entours, et s'élève,
  Et sans pitié dévore sa beauté,
    Ses dixhuit ans, hélas, et son beau rêve ! "
        Casimir de la Vigne, *La Toilette de Constance.*

[2] The Tay Bridge disaster Sunday, Dec. 28, 1879.

arraignment of nature, as though she were execrably ruthless, and execrably indifferent? [1] Not so, my brethren. Death whenever it comes is but death. None of us has any promise of this or that amount of life. It needs no railway accident, no sinking ship, or breaking ice, or burning town, or flame from heaven, or arrow in the darkness, or smiting of the sun by day, or the moon by night, to cut short our days. An invisible sporule in the air may do it, or a lesion no bigger that a pin's point.

> "He ate, drank, laughed, loved, lived, and liked life well;
> Then came—who knows?—some gust of jungle wind,
> A stumble on the path; a taint i' the tank;
> A snake's nip; half a span of angry steel;
> A chill; a fishbone; or a falling tile,—
> And life is over, and the man is dead."

But is this any reason why we should look on ourselves as victims of dead irresponsible forces?

---

[1] I allude, of course, to Mr. J. S. Mill's famous impeachment of nature in his posthumous Three Essays on Religion (pp. 28—36), in which among other things he says that Nature, "with the most supercilious disregard both of mercy and of justice," is guilty of deeds "such as the ingenious cruelty of a Nabis or a Domitian never surpassed."

Why so? death is but death, and, if we live faithfully, death is our richest birthright. The youth whom the girl he loved persuaded to go back to his duty by that fatal train last week, and who perished in it in a moment, must he not have died some day, could he have died better than in doing his duty? "Were you ready to die that you jumped into the stormy sea to save that child's life?" said a gentleman to an English sailor. "Should I have been better prepared, sir," the sailor answered, "if I had shirked my duty?" A sudden death is often, and in many respects, the most merciful form of death; and the apparently terrible death of a few may save the lives of many hundreds. The uniformity of nature may sometimes wear the aspect of passionless cruelty; but as we learn more and more to observe and to obey her laws, we find more and more that they work for countless ends of beneficence and beauty, that out of *seeming* evil she works real good, out of *transient* evil enduring good. The fires which rend the earthquake and burst from the volcano, are the quickening forces of the world; her storms lash the lazy atmosphere which otherwise would stagnate into pestilence, and it is for man's blessing, not for his destruction, that her waters roll and her great winds blow.

3. But are we, after all, so very helpless before the aggregate of these mighty forces, as materialism loves to represent? Not so! "Thou madest him to have dominion over the works of thy hands," said the Psalmist, "Thou hast put all things under his feet." "Replenish the earth, and subdue, and have dominion," said the first utterance of God to man. And what is this but an equivalent of the latest utterances of science, that "the order of nature is ascertainable by our faculties to an extent which is practically unlimited, and that our volition counts for something in the course of events"?[1] Man has done much to make the world in all senses a worse place for himself, but he has also,

---

[1] Huxley, *Lay Sermons*, p. 159.

thank God, done much to make it better, and he may, to an almost unspeakable extent, remedy for himself and for his race the throes and agonies of the groaning universe. God meant His earth to be a more blessed place for us than it is, and in every instance men have made it more blessed when they have read the open secrets, by virtue of which, for our incitement, if not for our reward, 'herbs have their healing, stones their preciousness, and stars their times.' Ancient nations have shuddered at the awfulness of the *Sea*. It drowns ship and sailor; but "trim your sail, and the same wave which drowns the barque is cleft by it, and bears it along like its own foam, a plume and a power." The *Lightning* shatters tower and temple; but once learn that it is nothing but the luminous all-pervading fluid which you may evolve by rubbing a piece of amber, and brush out of a child's fair hair, and then with no more potent instrument than a boy's kite you may dash harmless to the earth the all-shattering brand which was the terror of antiquity,[1] nay, you may seize it by its wing of fire, and bid it carry your messages around the girdled globe. *Zymotic diseases* smite down the aged and the young, but, when you have learnt that they are caused by myriads of invisible germs which float in the water or the air, you have but to observe the commonest rules of sanitary science, to filter and boil the dangerous water, to insure free currents of air, to breathe as nature meant you to breathe, through the nostrils, and not through the throat, and you rob them of half their deadliness. Why has Small-pox been stayed in its loathly ravages, and deprived of its hideous power? Why does the Black Death rage no longer, as it raged among the monks of this Abbey four centuries ago? Why do we not have Pestilence, like that great plague of London, which destroyed 7,165 persons in a

---

[1] " That blessed triumph when the patriot sage
Call'd the red lightnings from the o'er-rushing cloud,
And dash'd the beauteous terrors on the earth
Smiling majestic."—Coleridge, *Religious Musings*.

single week? Why has Gaol fever disappeared? Why are the cities of Europe horrified no longer by the hideousness of mediæval Leprosy? Because men live amid cleaner and purer surroundings. Because rushes are no longer strewn over floors which had been suffered to be saturated with the organic refuse of years. Because the simplest laws of nature are better understood. Because, in these respects, men have remedied by God's aid, some of those miseries for which the Saviour sighed.

4. And this amelioration of man's miseries is a great, and noble, and Christlike work. Would that there were no other side to the picture! Man, alas! also has done, and may do infinite mischief to the world he lives in. He may cut down the forests on the hills, and so diminish the necessary rain. He may pluck up the grasses on the shore, and so lay waste whole acres to the devastating sands. He may poison the sweet pure rivers of his native soil, till their crystal freshness is corrupted into deathful and putrescent slime. He may herd together, as we

suffer our poor to do, in filthy tenements which shall breed every species of disease and vice. He may indulge or acquiesce in senseless fashions and pernicious vanities which shall mean not only wasteful ugliness and grotesque extravagance, but even shattered health and ruined lives, to the mothers of his race. He may in greed of competition, extirpate the game of the forest, the fishes of the sea. He may destroy the exquisite balance of nature, by shooting down or entrapping the sweet birds of the air, till his vines and his harvests are devastated by the insects on which they feed. He may suffer the chimneys of his manufactories to poison the atmosphere with black smoke and sulphurous acid, till his proudest cities are stifled at noonday, as we all have seen in London for these many weeks, with the unclean mirk of midnight fogs. He may suffer noxious gases to be vomited upon the breeze, till the most glorious buildings in his cities corrode and crumble—as the stones of this Abbey are doing—under their influence,— till the green woods blacken into leafless wastes, and life is lived at miserable levels of vitality under the filthy reek. There is hardly any limit to the evil, no less than to the good, which man may do to this his earthly environment. Nor is it less deplorable that he may go out of his way to do endless mischief to himself, by his misuse or abuse of the properties of things. From the dried capsules of the white poppy he extracts opium, and he grows acres of poppies that with thousands of chests of that opium, he may degrade into decrepitude and wretchedness the most populous nation upon earth. Nature gives him the purple grape and the golden grain, and he mashes them and lets them rot and seethe, and assists, and superintends, and retards their decomposition, till he has educed from them a fermented intoxicating liquor; and not content with this as a luxury, he pours it into Circean cups of degrading excess; not content with even fermentation, he further, by distillation, extracts a transparent, mobile, colourless fluid, which is the distinctive element in ardent spirits and these, whatever may be their legitimate use in manufacture or in medicine, he has so horribly abused that they have become to mankind, the *spiritus ardentes* indeed, but not of heaven—fiery spirits of the abyss, which have decimated nations, ruined continents, shortened millions of lives, and turned for millions of God's children, and millions of Christ's little ones, life into an anguish, and earth into a hell. Do not say we can do nothing to soften for man the deadly agencies which are working in the world,—for all this mischief, and incalculably more than this, is man's own doing.

> "God made the living soul,
> The ruined creature is the work of man."

5. But in this attempt to show you that we have Christ's work to do for the groaning creation, I will not leave you with only this dark specimen of infatuation and misuse. Rather let me ask you to glance for a moment at one of the *beneficent* secrets which nature has yielded up to man. Have you ever realised, with heartfelt gratitude to God, the priceless boon which He has granted to this generation

in the diminution of pain? One of our best surgeons has just told us the strange yet simple story of this discovery, from the first dim intimation of the possibility in 1798, till in 1846 it might almost be said that in Europe we could name the month, before which all operative surgery was agonising, and after which it was painless.[1] But what an immense, what an enormous boon is this application of anodynes! "Past all counting is the sum of happiness enjoyed by the millions who have, in the last thirty-three years, escaped the pain that was inevitable in surgical operations; pain made more terrible by apprehension; more keen by close attention; sometimes awful in a swift agony; sometimes prolonged beyond even the most patient endurance, and then renewed in memory, and terrible in dreams. This will never be felt again." And besides this abolition of pain, it would take long to tell how chloroform and ether "have enlarged the field of useful surgery, making many things

[1] Sir James Paget, in the *Nineteenth Century*, Dec. 1879.

easy which were difficult, many safe which were perilous, many practical which were nearly impossible." Of the discoverers—mainly four—it is a lesson not without its religious significance, that one alone had earthly rewards,—Sir James Simpson, whose bust is in this Abbey. Of the other three, two,—such are earth's rewards if we work for them!—two died after years of worry and disappointment, insane and by their own hand, leaving their families in poverty; the third, without wealth or honours, is living, and is in an asylum now. But another lesson this eminent man of science draws, which bears directly on our subject;—that while we are profanely decrying nature, discoveries the most blessed, boons the most priceless, may lie close to us and yet God leave us to discover them; and that we may endure many needless miseries, falsely accusing nature and even God, only because we have neither hope enough to excite intense desire, nor desire enough to encourage hope. We wonder that for forty years the discovery of anæsthetics was not pursued, though, after the pregnant hint of Sir H. Davy, it lay but half hidden under so thin a veil. Our successors will wonder at us, as we at those before us, that we were as blind to who can tell how many great truths, which, they will say, were all around us, within reach of any clear and earnest mind. They will wonder at the quietude with which we stupidly acquiesce in, or immorally defend, the causes which perpetuate and intensify our habitual miseries. Our fathers needlessly put up with these miseries "as we now put up with typhoid fever and sea-sickness; with local floods and droughts; with waste of health and wealth in pollutions of rivers; with hideous noises, and foul smells;" with the curse of alcoholic poisoning, and many other miseries. Our successors when they have remedied or prevented these, will look back on them with horror, and on us with wonder and contempt, for what they will call our idleness or blindness, or indifference to suffering. Alas! in the physical as in the moral world, we murmur at the evils which surround us, and we do not remove them. We multiply those evils, and make life wretched, and then curse nature because it *is* wretched, and neglect or fling away the precious gifts, and easy remedies which would make it blest. And is it not so in the spiritual world? Nine-tenths of our miseries are due to our sins. Yet the remedy of our sins is close at hand. We have a Saviour; we have been commemorating His birth; but we live and act as though He were dead; in our own lives and those of others we suffer those miseries to run riot which He came to cure; we talk and live as though those remedies were undiscoverable, while from day to day His Word is very nigh us, even in our mouths and in our hearts!

6. I had intended to pass on to those aspects of the subject which perhaps you might consider to be more immediately religious, more directly practical; but these I must now leave till another Sunday. Nor am I altogether sorry. We dwarf religion as we dwarf everything else. We make it hard, narrow, selfish, Pharisaic, exclusively individual. We breathe upon its glorious

ideal, and it fades. With our sectarian dogmatism we clutch its opening buds of hope, and they wither "like a garland in a Fury's grasp." O how have we sinned—we who are set apart to be its teachers, ourselves, every one of us, terribly needing to be taught!—how have we sinned by making men suppose that religion is to be identified with scholasticism; that a man may be scorned and pitied as a heretic if he happen to lose his way in a labyrinth of theosophic technicalities. How have we sinned so far as we have left men to suppose that what we call religion delights in railing and heresy-hunting; that its right hand does but grasp the thunders of human anathemas; that we can look with remorseless hallelujahs on millions of the perishing, so that we save our individual souls! We may profess to repudiate such language now, but there it stands in all its horror on the pages of theologians. O how have we sinned— Churches sinned, priests sinned, preachers sinned —in leading men to suppose that the visitation of God means some stroke of wrath and vengeance, not the never-failing mercies of His fatherly providence, not the all-embracing tenderness of His illimitable love! Keble in his hymn on the sigh of Christ has said,

> " The deaf may hear the Saviour's voice,
>   The fettered tongue its chain may break
> But the deaf heart, the dumb by choice,
>   The laggard soul that will not wake,
> The guilt that scorns to be forgiven,
> These baffle e'en the spells of heaven;
> In thought of these His brows benign
> Not e'en in healing cloudless shine."

But who is responsible too often for the deaf ear, the fettered tongue, the deaf heart, the laggard soul, the defiant guilt? Is it not the blind guidance of the blind? Is it not the deaf heart of the hard religionist? Against whom was it that the indignation of the Saviour burned with so fierce a flame? Read the Four Gospels for yourselves, and see. Was it against the poor wretched sinners—the drunkards, the publicans, the harlots, the people who knew not the law and were accursed, the ignorant heathen, the grossly unorthodox Samaritan? or was it against sleek Scribes, who made religion repellent with harsh dogmas and burdensome ceremonials; against rich respectable Pharisees; against those that accounted themselves righteous and despised others; against men who lived in the odour of their own sanctity, amid the self-approving beatitudes of mutual benedictions? My brethren, amid your morbid self-introspections will you never look upwards? will nothing short of a thunderclap make you notice that heaven is blue? Will you always stare on the sea of glass mingled with fire before the throne, and never at the rainbow which spans it round? I am glad that I have, for once at any rate, preached you a sermon which is not solely about your individual souls. Individualism, dogmatism, sectarianism, religious party,—shall we, amid the clamours and condemnations of these, never learn that God is love? that the Gospel of Christ is a Gospel of "good will towards men?" Sin is terrible enough; the punishment of sin is terrible enough. It is the falsehood, sometimes of stupidity, sometimes of malice, to say that I have ever denied that there is a punishment for sin both here and hereafter. There is such punishment, and it will be, as it now is, terribly exceedingly. So far from dogmatising or rashly intruding into unrevealed mysteries, what I have done—driven thereto by the agonies of certain death-beds—is only to *refuse* to dogmatise where Scripture is silent or to clear away untenable renderings and traditional misinterpretations from its recorded words. But now from the inferential speculations of theology I would call you to another set of thoughts, even to these,—God is love, His purpose is love; if many of us are lost, He sent His Son to seek and save His lost; if His sheep wander into the wilderness, the Good Shepherd in the Parable searches for His sheep, until He find them. Why? because He grieves over human sin, and pities human misery. And therefore to remedy evil, to strive for good,—not to neglect the little daily duties and beneficences of life, the gracious acts, the tender courtesies, the tolerant appreciations, the public magnanimities, the social efforts, the national aims of nobler manhood, either in selfish absorption in the effort to save our own souls, or in fury against others because they will not save their souls in our way,—in one word to love God and our neighbour, and to believe on the name of Jesus Christ, and to love one another as He gave us commandment,—this is to live as Christ lived on earth. Let us do our work, and let Popes, and Sadducees, and Pharisees, and Inquisitors, say their say. It may be that there is danger sometimes for the humanitarian, the philanthropist, the reformer, lest in vast strivings for the good of others he forget that the motive power and purifying element of such work can only lie in personal devotion to his Saviour, in personal communion with his God. "Are you not afraid of neglecting your own soul amid your labours for the negroes?" asked one, of Clarkson, the abolitionist. "I leave God to take care of my soul while I do His work," was the reply. On the lips of a truly good man, it was a noble reply. It was like Moses, "Oh, these people have sinned—yet now if thou wilt forgive their sin,—and if not, blot me, I pray thee, out of thy book." It is St. Paul, "I could have wished my own self to be anathema from Christ, for the sake of my brethren, my kinsmen according to the flesh." It is Whitefield's, "Let the name of George Whitefield perish, if God be glorified." In a different region from that of the spiritual life it is even Danton's "Let my name be branded so France be free." The true Christian knows or may know that there is no antithesis, but the deepest sympathy between his divine inner life, and his vigorous outward usefulness; that his work will be most blessed when his heart is most merciful and pure; that his holiest prayers will transform themselves into his happiest labours; and that while he serves God better by giving a cup of cold water in His name to one of His little ones than though he weekly partook of seven fasting but loveless communions, he will still need the cry

> "O perfect pattern from above,
> So strengthen us that ne'er
> Prayer keeps us back from works of love,
> Or works of love from prayer."

But for one sermon you hear about work for the secular amelioration of the suffering world for which Christ sighed, you may (I suppose) hear fifty on passing ecclesiastical controversies and five thousand about individual efforts for personal salvation. And yet one pure, self-sacrificing deed, one word of generosity to an opponent, one kindly act to aid another, may have been better for you in God's sight, and far far harder for you to do, than to attend in the year the 730 daily services which this Abbey provides. Yes, I am glad that I have preached to you to-day the duty of what some would call secular work—as though secular work were not often the most profoundly religious work!—for the amelioration of the world. And I say, that it were better for you to have made but two blades of grass grow where one grew before, than if, with the hollow, hateful, slanderous heart of some of the false prophets of modern religionism, you were every morning to do whatever modern thing may be analogous to binding your fringes with blue, and broadening your phylacteries,—to making the hill-tops blaze with your sacrificial fires, building here seven altars, and offering a bullock and a ram on every altar. And so, my brethren, let us leave this Abbey to-day with conceptions of duty larger and more hopeful; with more yearning both after the sympathy of Christ and after His activity; with more faith to see that the world would not be so utter a ruin but for our perversity; with more hope to be convinced that even we can help to redeem its disorders, and restore its pristine perfectness. Let us obey the command, "Ephphatha, Be opened!" Let us lift up our eyes to see that, though the air around us is colourless, the far-off heaven is blue. Let us see and be thankful for the beauty of the world, the sweet air, the sunshine, the sea, the splendid ornaments of heaven, the ever-recurring circles of the divine beneficence. Let us learn the secrets of the mighty laws which only crush us when we disobey them, and which teach us, with divine inflexibility, that as we sow we reap. Let us not hinder the students of science in their patient toil and marvellous discovery by the crude infallibilities of our ignorant dogmatism. Let us believe—for we were saved in Hope—that "Utopia itself is but another word for time;" and that, if our own work seems but infinitesimal, yet "there are mites in science, as well as in charity, and the ultimate results of each are alike important and beneficial."[1] And so the more we share in the sigh and in the toil of the Saviour, the more shall we share in His redeeming gladness,—the more shall we see and share in

> "The joy of God to see a happy world."

If we be Christians at all, we are all joining, or trying to join, somehow, in the one great Psalm of life. To one who hears it near at hand many of our notes may seem hideous and most discordant; but a little farther off in time

[1] Dr. Richardson's *Hygeia*.

and space, as with a Scotch psalm amid the mountains, "the true notes alone support one another, all following the one true rule; the false notes, each following its own false rule, quickly destroy one another, and the psalm, which was discordant enough near at hand, is a perfect melody when heard from far."[1] Oh that our lives might add to the dominant melody; might help to subdue and drown those disproportionate and jarring notes!

[1] T. Carlyle.

SERMON VI.

THE MENDING AND MARRING OF HUMAN LIFE.

THE MENDING AND MARRING OF HUMAN LIFE.

Pour out, we beseech Thee, O Lord, Thy spirit of grace upon us Thy servants, and cast out from us whatever evil we have incurred by the fraud of the devil, or by earthly corruption, that, being cleansed within and without, we may ever render unto Thee a pure worship, through Jesus Christ our Lord. Amen.

> "A sacred burthen is this life ye bear,
> Look on it, lift it, bear it solemnly,
> Stand up, and walk beneath it steadfastly.
> Fall not for sorrow, falter not for sin,
> But onward, upward, till the goal ye win."
>
> F. A. KEMBLE.

SERMON VI.

THE MENDING AND MARRING OF HUMAN LIFE.

Hos. xiii. 9.

"*O Israel thou hast destroyed thyself, but in me is thine help.*"

OUR subject on these Sundays, my friends, has been the amelioration of the world. We have seen that if our Lord sighed before He opened the blind eyes, He sighed because He grieved over the sorrows of man on earth, and that His grief took form in the sacrifice of His own life, that we—our bodies, souls, and spirits—might share in His great salvation. If then this was the idea of His life—deep sympathy expressing itself in noble toil—it ought to be the idea of ours; and we have tried to see how, both in the material world, and in the world of sin and sorrow, we may do very much, both actively and passively—both by diminishing the miseries of mankind, and by abstaining from the aggravation of them—to make man's life happier than it is. We tried last Sunday to glance at the truth that even the laws and conditions of the material creation might be so used as to avert their severity and turn them into unbounded blessings; and that half the evils which afflict the nations are created by their own perversity, springing, as they do, from abused blessings, or conditions which they themselves deprave. And surely all these are deeply religious considerations. Every good man, every man who sincerely desires to be a soldier and servant of Jesus Christ, should be glad to devote every gift and faculty which he possesses to the service of his brethren for whom Christ died.

It is only because we are all so naturally and intensely selfish that the broader aspects of this truth—those which affect our natural life, or our general relation to the world in which we live—always seem to be regarded as less immediately profitable. But (still keeping it in view as our object to see in what ways God desires us to make all life happier), let us consider to-day our *individual* lives and see whether they would not furnish fewer causes for the Saviour's sigh if we would but keep steadily in sight the great purposes of God respecting us. Are there not two main ways in which we might do this—the one by making fuller and more thankful use of the innocent blessings which God's bounty has lavished upon us; the other by not ruining and destroying our own selves, as we do when we poison the very springs of natural and spiritual joy by the introduction of alien elements into our bodies and our souls?—We suffer by misdoing; we suffer by neglect.

1. I say then, first, that we suffer by neglect. The full, rich, innocent use of gifts and opportunities—how little do we understand it! For every purpose of noble gladness, how much more might almost every one of us make of our life than we do! How do we throw away the substance for the shadow, and the healthy

reality for the feverish dream! How do we crowd out the natural effects, and make all life artificial. We spend our life, as it were, on the stage and under the gaslight, when we might be walking in the sunlight under heaven. We talk of poverty and limitation, while we make life "a haggard, malignant, running for luck," and are daily neglecting the elements of purest and loftiest pleasure. "Give me," says an American writer, "health and a day, and I will make the pomp of emperors ridiculous." But to enable us thus to enjoy the gifts of nature we all need more open eyes, more grateful hearts. I often think that most of us in life are like many of those sightseers who saunter through this Abbey. Their listless look upon its grandeur and its memorials, furnishes an illustration of the aspect which we present to higher powers, as we wander restlessly through the solemn minster-aisles of life. For this Abbey appeals in different ways to different feelings. There are some, who with no special knowledge or education, have yet a heart to feel at once the genius of the place. Its grandeur and solemnity strike into them an involuntary awe. For them

> "Bubbles burst, and Folly's dancing foam
> Melts as they cross the threshold."

They feel as even the puritan Milton felt when he spoke of the "high-embowèd roof," the massy pillars, the storied windows, the pealing organ, the full-voiced choir, the solemn Psalms. They have at least the innate sense of what is great, and, amid these ugly wildernesses of brick, the Abbey, blackened as it is by the smoke and fog which hangs over this city year by year, and with its battlements and stones corroded by the sulphurous acids of the air, still speaks to them in a nobler language than they hear in the shops and streets. Others, who have some knowledge of Architecture, can exult in each exquisite detail of sculpture, each harmony of proportion, each impress of the thought of those ages of faith to which these cathedrals of England owe their origin. Others have a deep interest in History, and the memorials around us seem to give them a deeper comprehension, and a more living union with the past. Others again, thrill with sympathy as they stand among the tombs of the mighty dead, and amid these records of past lives they hear in its softest tones, "the sad music of humanity." But when all these feelings are combined, then a visit to the Abbey leaves those rich and vivid impressions of delight and elevation which you may find recorded in the descriptions of an Addison, a Washington Irving, or a Macaulay. How is it then that myriads who come here do but look round with dreary indifference and listless vacancy, while they would be roused to an enthusiasm of delight by the buffoonery of a comic singer, or the horrible fling of an acrobat on a trapeze? To them as to the most gifted the Abbey presents the same outward appearance; the same vision strikes their retina. But the eye can only see what it brings with it the power of seeing. The difference is in *them*, and mostly through no fault of theirs. They have neither the sense of beauty, nor the knowledge of art, nor the feeling for history, nor the interest in noble lives, which should make these walls speak to them. Music can be nothing to the deaf ear; nor the glories of the sunset to the blind eye; nor the highest utterances of poetry to the ignorant, dead, and callous heart. To them that have is it given, and they have more abundantly.

Even so it is with life, with the temple of the outward world. We talk of human misery; how many of us derive from life one-tenth part of what God meant to be its natural blessedness? How many of us drink the deep draughts of joy which every pure heart may drink out of the river of His pleasures? Sit out in the open air on a summer day, and how many of us have trained ourselves to notice the sweetness and the multiplicity of the influences which are combining for our delight—the song of birds; the breeze beating balm upon the forehead; the genial warmth; the delicate odour of ten thousand flowers; the play of lovely colours; "the soft eye-music of slow-waving boughs?" How many of us ever watch the pageant of the clouds, or take in the meaning of a starry night, or so much as see the sunrise? Or if we do, is not the remark of the poor poet-painter true of us, "When the sun rises you see something like a golden guinea coming out of the sea: I see and hear likewise an innumerable company of angels praising God." How many of us, notice, as loving and gifted observers might help us to notice, the multitudinous beauty and tenderness of the burst of spring; the black ashbuds in March; the glistening chestnut-buds in April; the blaze of celandines; the golden dust in the catkins of the hazel; the rosy sheath of the larch-tree's fresh green leaves. A poet speaks of one to whom

> "A primrose by a river's brim,
> A yellow primrose was to him,
> And it was nothing more."

He means by those lines to express the difference between bare sight and divine insight; between the cold unfurnished sensual soul, and the soul that sees the Unseen, sees God in all things, and sees all things in God. Truly "the misery of man appears like childish petulance, when we explore the steady and prodigal provision which has been made for his support and delight on this green ball that floats him through the universe."

> "More servants
> Wait on man than he'll take notice of."

We all live on far lower levels of vitality and of joy than we need to do. We linger in the misty and oppressive valleys when we might be climbing the sunlit hills. God puts into our hands the Book of Life, bright on every page with open secrets, and we suffer it to drop out of our hands unread.

2. Even this negative side of the subject is of course a boundless one. If we suffer from limitation of the insight which would open our blind souls to myriads of happy impressions, how do we suffer also—all mankind alike— from the neglect of our own powers! Our

capacities — and the full exercise of every capacity is a source of happiness — largely exceed our attainments. No nation has ever desired to train a particular faculty of man without finding that faculty capable of indefinite development. Why does the wild Indian track his path with unerring certainty through the interminable forest? Why was there no limit to the hardy endurance of the Spartan boy? Why was the young Athenian a model of grace, agility, and beauty? Why can the Arab tell you the number of approaching horsemen where you barely see a speck on the horizon? Why do the muscles stand out so strong upon an athlete's arm? The faculties, the gifts are there—they are a part of our natural heritage—but they lie undeveloped in us all. They perish for lack of training, and become as though they were not. We talk of education; we call this an age of education. For myself, I doubt—such poor blind creatures are we at the best—whether, after millenniums of its existence, the human race has grasped one-tenth part of the secrets of education; whether many of our aims and methods in education are not deplorably foolish; whether while aiming at our fineries of Latin Verse and other trivialities, we have not grievously retrograded from sensible ideals; whether much of our so-called highest education is not—in comparison with much that we might do—an elaborate missing of the mark. At any rate who shall venture to say that, in the use of our blessings, in the training of our powers, we have as a race attained to anything like what we might be, or done even a fraction of what we might do? Far better and brighter is the world than we will see, or suffer it to be for us; far more rich in capabilities of power and blessedness than we have made them are the immortal souls which God has given us, the mortal bodies into whose nostrils He has breathed the breath of life.

3. That, then, is the negative side of the matter—what we cannot see, what we will not do; but alas! the positive side is far more humiliating. Man complains of his misery

on earth; but "this," it has been said, "we may discover assuredly; this every true light of science, every mercifully-granted power, every wisely-restricted thought may teach us more clearly day by day, that in the heavens above, and in the earth beneath, there is one continual and omnipotent Presence of life, and of peace, for all who know that they live, and remember that they die." Alas! do we not, too often, and too many of us, live as though we should never die to earth, and die as though we should never live beyond it? Do we not make of life a living death till we have sunk so low that the best boon for us might well seem to be an everlasting oblivion?

And that is why life is so full of misery— misery of body, misery of mind.

We should all admit at once that a very large portion of that misery of man for which our Lord sighed was the result of diseased conditions of body; and men often talk as though bodily disease were a part of the spite and cruelty of nature. Ah! my friends, how vast a part of human disease results, not only as we have seen from the ignorance, but also from the folly and the sin of man. Typhoid, and leprosy, and the black death, small-pox, and gaol fever, are not by any means the only diseases which might be almost, if not quite, eliminated from among us. We talk with deep self-pity of the ravages of gout, and cancer, and consumption, and mental alienation. Alas! how many of these might in one or two generations cease to be, if we all lived the wise and temperate and happy lives which nature meant us to lead! And the voice of nature rightly interpreted is ever the voice of God. Even the simplest of us are superfluous in our demands, and the vast majority of men so live as, more or less habitually, to pamper the appetite with wasteful extravagance, and weaken the health by baneful luxuries. By unwholesome narcotics, by burning and adulterated stimulants, by many and highly-seasoned meats, by thus storing the blood with unnatural elements, which it cannot assimilate, they clog and carnalise the aspirations which they should cherish, and feed into uncontrollable force the many-headed monster of the passions which they should control. Hence it is that millions of lives are like sweet bells jangled out of tune, and however pompous may be the epitaphs upon their tombs, millions of men in these days, like the Israelites of old, are laid to rest in *Kibroth Hattaavah*—the graves of lust.

And the sad thing is that this heavy punishment ends not with the individual. It is not only that the boy, when he has marred his own boyhood, hands on its moral results to the youth; and the youth, when he has marred them yet more irretrievably, hands them on to the man that he may finish the task of that perdition;—but alas! the man also hands them on to his innocent children, and they are born with bodies tormented with the disproportionate impulses, sickly with the morbid cravings, enfeebled by the increasing degeneracy, tainted by the retributive disease of guilty parents. And all this disorder has arisen because the weaker and baser elements of our nature have been endowed with a force which is the result, not of God's original design for man, but of man's violation of those high laws which He designed for our guidance and our protection. But in spite of these trials God does not mean us to be disheartened. Those laws of His to which we give the name of nature, have in them a strong recuperative force; they tend back from the degeneracy to the original perfection; they are ever working for the restoration of powers not irretrievably impaired, for the renewal of harmonies which have not yet been made hopelessly discordant. In one sense, indeed, it is terribly true that there is vicarious suffering: that the fathers eat sour grapes and the children's teeth are set on edge; but while, on the one hand, we cease to perplex ourselves with the solution of that side of the mystery which we cannot solve, let us, on the other, see for our comfort that, in spite of man's defection and self-destruction, God is most merciful and most just. If any of you are at this moment suffering in your own persons from the sins of your parents, it may be only because He would grant to you a more glorious victory, a more infinite reward. Let us take but one instance. There are men living now—physicians tell us of them—to whom, in bitter legacy, their fathers have bequeathed so fierce and mad a craving for stimulants, that they have felt as if a dead hand out of the abyss were ever clutching at them as with a grasp of fire. And yet such men, though for them the conditions of life have been made so perilous, have by the grace of God completely triumphed. In daily battle, armed in the armour of righteousness, they have done all and stood, and by their side, like an unsleeping sentinel, the strong angel of conscience has kept guard, quenching on the shield of faith shower after shower of the fiery darts of the wicked one. Those men are true heroes; and though they may die obscure, though man may know nothing of their noble struggles, for them "all the trumpets shall sound on the other side."

And there are inherited impulses worse if possible than even this;—conditions of disease, mental, physical, and moral, which have been perpetuated by the unlawful pleasure whereof the end is deathful corruption. It is a touching story of the late Archbishop Whately, that, when he lay in agony on his deathbed, his chaplain tried to comfort him with the words, "Who shall change our vile body." "Read it," he said. The chaplain read the passage from our English Bible. "Read it," said the dying Archbishop, "in his own words." The chaplain read it in the Greek, and there the words literally are, "Who shall change the body of our humiliation." "Ah!" said Dr. Whately, "that is it; nothing that God has made is *vile*."[1] No, our bodies are not vile; but they are, alas, too often bodies of humiliation—of humiliation deepened into abjectness by the sins of others or our own. There are mysteries in our moral nature, my brethren, on which we dare not dwell; to which

---

[1] Phil. iii. 21. ὃς μετασχηματίσει τὸ σῶμα τῆς ταπεινώσεως ἡμῶν.

in the pulpit it is scarcely possible even to allude. But can any man grow to manhood without becoming aware how many poison their own life-blood with a sore degradation which is God's executioner on those who force their way through the resistances and admonitions of law and conscience to pluck the forbidden fruit of sensual pleasure? If any young man who has been walking after his own heart's lusts, feels in consequence one touch of the avenging finger of violated law—is he really unaware that such a taint in the blood may prove to be, and that not for one generation only, the afflictive curse of even the most innocent lives? Oh, my brethren, if men would but make a more serious effort to live, as they were taught by their catechisms to live, in temperance, soberness, and chastity; to live as they pray in their prayers to live, a righteous, sober, and godly life; to live as all wise men have urged us to live, in "plain living and high thinking;" to live as nature teaches us to live, by the rule of "not too much;" to live as Scripture urges us to live, "not in rioting and drunkenness, not in chambering and wantonness, not in strife and envying;"—and how much more if we would but strive to live by "putting on the Lord Jesus Christ, and making no provision for the flesh to fulfil the lusts thereof:"—how vast a change would even one single generation see in the health, the happiness, the ennoblement of mankind! And if we could, by energy, and faithfulness, and earnest prayer for the aid of God's Holy Spirit, teach but the youth of one generation that the sowing of the wind means always the reaping of the whirlwind; that each man is mainly what he makes himself; that there is an inevitable congruity between the seed and the fruit; that he who would be truly courageous, who would dare all things, who would be a benefactor of his race, who would look unabashed into the face of all mankind though they were arrayed together to crush him, who would achieve the highest purposes of his reason and the most generous ideals of his soul,—that he who, though he sternly mastered his passions, would combine calmness and peace with force and fire, whose life would be a poem though he wrote none,—that he who would live as one "who loves all beauty whether of nature or of art, and hates all vileness, and respects others as himself," and whose life as it draws its strength from holy inspiration so spends that strength in devoted service; if, I say, we could teach the youth of but one generation that he who would do thus, and be this, "must retain from his earliest youth, and in the most secret sessions of his memory, a spotless title to self-respect," by a pure, a self-denying, and a holy life; then how soon would these mortal bodies of ours, these harps of a thousand strings, not only keep in tune, but ring with the very melodies of heaven! Then would the nations grow in strength, in health, in nobleness, and would eliminate from among themselves, each man for himself, and all by united allegiance to the interests of their race, not a few out of that multiplicity of afflictions for which Christ sighed, and from which He came to set us free; then should old age be like that described by our great poet—

> "For in my youth I never did apply
> Hot and rebellious liquors in my blood;
> Nor did not with unbashful forehead woo
> The means of weakness and debility;
> Therefore mine age is as a lusty winter,
> Frosty, but kindly."

Old age should be like this, and death should be like the dropping of ripe fruit from the tree;—say rather, like a sleep sent by God to His beloved when their day's work is done—a sleep which shall awake amid the eternal realities of heaven. Is this a path worth the efforts of mankind to walk in? It was described long ago: "And an highway shall be there, and a way, and it shall be called The way of holiness; the unclean shall not pass over it; but it shall be for those: the wayfaring men, though fools, shall not err therein. No ravenous beast shall go up thereon; but the redeemed shall walk there: they shall obtain joy and gladness, and sorrow and sighing shall flee away."

4. But, in conclusion, my brethren, some of you

may say, You have but spoken to-day of the redemption, the amelioration, the improvement of the body, and our miseries are not of the body. We have health enough; we have not been intemperate; we are not thus impure. Yet we are restless, uneasy, troubled, smarting, some of us, under the world's gross injustice; troubled, some of us, by false tongues, tormented by delusive and frustrate hopes.

> " Canst thou not minister to a *mind* diseased,
> And with some sweet oblivious antidote
> Cleanse the stuffed bosom of that perilous stuff
> Which weighs upon the heart ?"

My brethren, in this matter no earthly antidote, no poppy nor mandragora of earth will help you; but there are such antidotes if you would minister them to yourselves. There is balm in Gilead; there is a physician there. If indeed you have a sound and pure body, then the victory over care is already half won. Mind and body are closely associated. A diseased or disordered body tends to make a troubled mind, for if you "rumple the jerkin you rumple also the jerkin's lining." Very many of our cares are but vapours, imaginary miseries, morbid egotisms, the thick intoxicating fumes of smouldering vanities. But a sound body goes far to make a sound mind, and oh, what an exquisite gift is—or must I say "might have been"?—the mind which God has given us. What a blue sky with not a cloud to sully it in infancy; how bright, and clear, and sunny in youth; what a picture gallery of glorious imagery in manhood; what a hallowed temple in old age, with the light of heaven streaming into it from above! How many of our minds are like this? Alas! where is even the temple into which foul things do not sometimes intrude? Is there no one here who must rather feel that his mind is more like a cage of unclean birds, darkened with the obscene wings which haunt the twilight? Do we want more than daily experience to show us in how many minds the "sick beast of envy" makes its lair? Are there many of us even here who are not suffering from, who are not weakened by, that disease of the age—care, fret, worry, over-work, over-competition, over-anxiety, over-haste to get rich, over-esteem for the transient and perishing treasures of earth? And in this case too, my friends, we suffer mainly from our own faults. Most of these our sufferings are self-inflicted. We are cruel to ourselves. We feather the arrows of our enemies, and make the wounds rankle, which otherwise they were powerless to inflict. We anticipate misfortunes which never come. We brood over injuries at which it would have been far wiser to smile. We neglect or despise the joys which God otherwise would freely give us. We will not know the things which make for our peace, and in things which we know naturally, like brute beasts made to be taken and destroyed, in these we corrupt ourselves. Ah, how true, how true it is that Heaven seems to be "everywhere if we would but enter it, and yet almost nowhere, because so few of us can." Alas, my brethren, all this might be otherwise, but as we ruin our bodies by excess and ignorance, so we ruin our minds by greed and care.

> " O purblind race of miserable men,
> How many among us at this very hour
> Do forge a lifelong trouble for ourselves,
> By taking true for false, or false for true,
> Here through the feeble twilight of the world
> Groping, how many, until we pass and reach
> That other where we see as we are seen ! "

Have you never observed, my brethren, that, in God's great goodness, even at far lower levels than those of spiritual religion, we might do very very much to lead happier and better lives, and so give to our loving Saviour less cause to sigh? It is not only from the heights of *religious* rapture that the poets sing,

> " My mind to me a kingdom is ;
> Such perfect joy therein I find,
> That it excells all other bliss
> Which God or nature hath assigned ; "

or again the noble lyric—

> " How happy is he born and taught
> Who serveth not another's will,
> Whose armour is his honest thought,
> And simple truth his utmost skill."

Clear thoughts, bright deeds, a simple, healthy life, a firm and tender nature, candour, charity, self-forgetfulness, unaffected delicacy, all that distinguishes the gentleman from the churl, all that distinguishes the pure from the polluted, all that distinguishes the liberal from the niggardly, these secrets of a mind at ease,—the secrets of that alchemy which can secure every grain of veritable gold which life has to offer, and precipitate its dross,—are not beyond the reach of even an enlightened heathen, an Epictetus or an Aurelius. But when beside all this a man is a Christian, then indeed

> "He that hath light within his own clear breast,
> May sit i' the centre and enjoy clear day."

Why do even we who profess and call ourselves Christians make our minds miserable by care and envy as we make our bodies miserable by sin? God gives us bread, and we turn it into a stone. We drive away from us our best friends and arm our enemies with scorpions.

And yet surely every one of us who has at all realised the central thoughts of Christianity, and the inner meaning of the Saviour's life, must feel that if not all forms of care, yet all those forms of earthly care which are most potent to make man wretched, *ought* to have been dispelled from the heart of him who has listened to the calm and loving invitation, "Come unto Me all ye that labour and are heavy laden, and I will give you rest."

Oh, my brethren, that we would win this blessedness! that we would learn these lessons! It is the life of the spirit which can alone make the mind noble and the body pure. Walk in the spirit, and ye shall not fulfil the lusts of the flesh. That joy of the Holy Ghost—even if it be born for us of darkness and tribulations, —is possible to us all. Let us not accuse nature or fate; nay, let us accuse ourselves. Are we unhappy? if so, may there be no cause for this in the pride which despises, the supineness which will not grasp, the blindness which will not see, the weakness and wickedness which deprave and defile the gifts of God? or may it not be that we are looking for happiness in wrong directions? or may it not be again, that we ought to be willing to resign *happiness* and look for *blessedness* instead? and are there any other secrets of blessedness but love to God and love to our neighbour? Why should we not try, each in our own little sphere, to make the world better for us, to utilise and subdue its forces, to expel its loathliest diseases, to centuple its noblest sources of happiness, to assuage its least tolerable pains? If this seem too grand an aim for our feebleness, can we not at least try to be ourselves humble and forgiving, diligent and faithful, kind and pure of heart? We can; we ought; all that we lack is the power to say we will. God gives that power as He gives all things else, seeing that He giveth His Holy Spirit to them that seek Him. The laws of nature are the laws of God, and the laws of God are beneficent laws. If man is so miserable, if all creation groans, if "the world's history is the world's judgment,"[1] it is because we refuse the lessons of nature, and violate the commandments of God. Oh, let us try to take away with us this lesson,—not only for ourselves individually, but in order better to serve our brethren,—that the laws of health, the laws of temperance, the laws of purity, the laws of contentment, will lead us straight back upon the road to the paradise of God; and that if, as we approach its gates, God's two great Angels of Reason and Conscience hold us by the hand, against the ingress of those high powers the flaming sword of the Cherubim will cease to wave; nay—the Avenging Cherubim will bow their heads before them; and, guided and blest, our path will lie straight onward to the Tree of Life.

[1] "Die Weltgeschichte ist das Weltgericht."
SCHILLER, *Resignation*.

SERMON VII.

LAST LESSONS FROM THE SIGH OF CHRIST.

LAST LESSONS FROM THE SIGH OF CHRIST.

O Almighty God, who alone canst order the unruly wills and affections of sinful men, grant unto Thy people that they may love the thing which Thou commandest, and desire that which Thou dost promise, that so among the sundry and manifold changes of the world our hearts may surely there be fixed where true joys are to be found, through Jesus Christ our Lord. Amen.

"And Thou, O Lord, by whom are seen
All creatures as they be;
Forgive me if too close I lean
My human heart on Thee."

SERMON VII.

MARK VII. 34.

"And looking up to heaven, He sighed, and saith unto him, Ephphatha, that is, Be opened."

I SHOULD be glad, my brethren, if to-day we could in any degree sum up and enforce that one main thought, which in its various applications has occupied us on these Sunday afternoons. For that reason, I end with the text with which I began and which suggested the considerations which we have tried to pass in review. Those considerations have never, I trust, for one moment lost sight of the one central truth of Christianity,—that the Lord Jesus Christ is our Light and our Life; the Word made flesh; the Son of God, the Saviour of the world. We believe that God is love, and we look to Jesus, the author and finisher of our faith, as to Him who revealed to us the inmost heart of God towards us. He, being in the form of God, came on earth to be a man with men; He taught us how to live, and made us not fear to die; He came to work out, by the one sacrifice of Himself once offered, a thousandfold redemption; to restore for us the broken harmonies of life; to ransom us from the thraldom of sin; to cast down Satan as lightning from heaven; to give power to all who receive Him that they should become the sons of God. It was, we believe, the cross of Christ which alone has made possible the amelioration of the world. Human nature, conquered, ruined, and debased, mastered by its lowest instincts, enslaved by its most dangerous passions, had, even apart from revelation, long dreamt of such a deliverer, and long yearned for him. We trace that yearning in Plato and in Virgil, in the despair of pagan philosophy and in the aspirations of pagan song.[1] We trace it even in those legends of the old mythology which were the unconscious

---

[1] Ἕως ἂν ὁ θεὸς αὐτός ἀπολύσῃ ἡμᾶς.—PLATO, *Phaed.* 379. (See Ackeronam, *Das Christliche im Plato*, pp. 21—75; Schneider,

prophecies of heathendom. That is one reason why so often in the catacombs the early Christians adopted Orpheus as the type of Christ —because the lyre of Orpheus made music through the world, tamed the savageness of the wild beasts, and lulled even the pangs of Erebus. In our own National Gallery you may see the splendid picture in which the greatest of English painters has given us from Greek legend another symbol of the work of Christ. It is Turner's picture of Apollo slaying the Python. Apollo was the god of life, of light, and of the sun; the python was the monster of midnight and corruption. That serpent monster, with his huge folds, crowds and darkens one whole side of the picture, crashing rocks and trees before him into frightful chaos, looking horrible in

---

Christliche Klänge, pp. 158, 244.) "Nemo per se satis valet ut emergat; oportet manum aliquis porrigat, aliquis educat."— SEN. *Ep.* 52. "Aliquem habeat animus quem vereatur, cujus auctoritate etiam secretum suum sanctius faciat."—ID. *Ep.* 11, 6. See Æsch. *Prom.* 1026—1030; Virg. *Ecl.* iv., &c. On this subject see Archbishop Trench's Hulsean Lectures, on the *Unconscious Prophecies of Heathendom.*

loathliness, yet irresistible in strength. On the other side of the picture kneels, bow in hand, a radiant figure,—the figure of the youthful sun-god; and, as his bowstring twangs, arrow after arrow of light hurtles into the monster's wounded bulk, and as you look closer you see that, for all his awfulness and strength, he is but bursting asunder in the midst, writhing vainly in the agonies of death. From his blood, indeed, as it streams forth, in one corner of the picture, is springing into life a little asp, which is darting away unnoticed. The intensely venomous gleam of that fiery serpent represents the heathen sense of despair, the painter's awful feeling of the apparently inextinguishable vitality of evil, the imperfection of deliverance, the unendingness of sin and anguish.[1] But in the promise of Paradise,

---

[1] The Python means THE CORRUPTER. "Apollo's contest with him in the strife of purity with pollution; of life with forgetfulness; of love with the grave... This dragon of decay is a mere colossal worm: wounded, he bursts asunder in the midst, and melts to pieces rather than dies, vomiting smoke—a smaller serpent-worm rising out of his blood. Alas for Turner!

when the work of the seed of the woman shall be completed, I nowhere see it said, that from the crushed head of the serpent shall break forth the cockatrice. In the new heaven and the new earth, in the restitution of all things, in the fresh creation of the world, when even the personified abstractions of shadowy beings —Death and Hades—have been flung into the lake of fire, we are told that there shall be no more curse, and that God shall be all in all. Let all men interpret these glorious promises of the future by such light as God may give them. I do not in the least care to question or dispute the limitations which others may feel compelled to attach to them. Our present thoughts are purely practical. We all alike agree that we see not yet all things put under Christ. We see that as yet the enemies are very strong which He has left it to us to conquer; the work

---

This smaller serpent-worm, it seemed, he could not conceive to be slain. In the midst of all the power and beauty of nature, he still saw this death-worm writhing amid the weeds . . . He was without hope."—RUSKIN, *Modern Painters*, v. 328.

very vast which He has bidden us carry to its close. Nearly nineteen centuries have sped away since the great Sacrifice was offered on Calvary, and we are living still in a world of error and ignorance, of misery and sin. And yet we do not despair. When the deep gloom settled down on Calvary, when the disciples had forsaken Him and fled, when priests and rulers, Jews and Gentiles, the soldiers and the mob, nay, even the crucified robbers at His side, had all been joining in insult and execration, when for one awful moment it seemed as if even His Father had forsaken Him, He, the Son of man and the Son of God, was still the Lord, the Victor, the Deliverer, and His " It is finished!" was the cry of triumph. That triumph, though still but partial, shall hereafter be universal. From the gloomy background of history, from the clouds and darkness which so often seem to settle down on our human lives, the eye of faith not only sees that cross stand out in holy light, but over it and around it we still read the name of Him who died thereon, and the promise of the vision which the first Christian emperor wove in letters of gold upon his labarum, "*By this thou shalt conquer!*"[1]

But the endurance of the cross was only the last act of the life of Christ; and we must look on that life as meant in every word of it for our enlightenment, in every act of it for our example. Not one of those acts was imperfect, not one of those words insignificant; and we have been trying to see what we could learn from the one act and word of our Lord when, with an upward glance of prayer, He sighed and said "*Ephphatha*," "be thou opened." That touch showed His miraculous power; that sigh His infinite compassion; that word His active intervention to heal the miseries which awoke His sorrow. Not to that poor sufferer only, but to us, to all mankind, He seems to say, "Thou art deaf, and canst not hear; dumb, and canst not

---

[1] " Christus purpureum gemmanti textus in auro
　　Signabat *labarum*, clipeorum insignia Christus
　　Scripserat: ardebat summis crux addita cristis."
　　　　　　　　—PRUDENT. *in Symmach.* ii. 484.

speak; thy whole being is closed, and hampered, and spoiled, and maimed; "*Ephphatha*, be thou opened; opened now at My word; opened completely and for ever!"[1] Rejoice, oh sinful, oh mourning, oh afflicted humanity! Let the eyes of the blind be opened and the ears of the deaf unstopped; let the lame man leap as a hart, and the tongue of the dumb sing, and say to them which are of fearful heart, *Fear not, be strong!*

This was the work and mission of Christ; and He has bidden us to carry it on. But it is useless, it is worse than useless, for it is an evil hypocrisy thus to say "Lord, Lord," yet not to do, or try to do the things which He says. It is a perilous falsehood to preach in His name, yet to have nothing of His spirit; to worship in His tabernacle, yet only to lay upon His altar the unhallowed incense of pride, and to kindle it with the fuming fire of vice and hate. If we truly love Him, if we love

---

[1] Such is the full meaning of διανοίχθητι.

one another as He gave us commandment, what have we to do in life? what must we *learn* from His sigh and from His act?

We might learn, my friends, far more than any or all of us can ever know, or see, or teach; but surely that small fragment of what we have tried to see on previous Sundays may be summed up in the three eternal duties of *compassion*, of *energy*, of *hope*.

1. We learn the duty of *compassion*. Is it a duty too obvious on which to dwell? Would to God it were as common in reality as it is in profession! There has been, and is, very little of true pity in the world. The world has in all ages deeply needed, and in this age still deeply needs, the lesson of pity. That the ancient heathen needed it amid their horrible cruelty and injustice to slaves and gladiators, and with their best philosophers ranking pity as a vice,[1] I need not stop to prove.[2] But the

---

[1] See Cic. *Tusc. Disp.* iv. 14, § 32.
[2] I have touched on this subject in my Hulsean Lectures, *The Witness of History to Christ*, pp. 98—114.

ancient Jew also needed it. Though there were in his Mosaic legislation divine lessons of mercy and tenderness, there was enough also of concession to ignorance and hardness of heart to make our Lord say, "Ye have heard that it hath been said, 'An eye for an eye, a tooth for a tooth,' but I say to you, that ye resist not evil. . . . Ye have heard that it hath been said . . . 'Thou shalt hate thine enemy,' but I say unto you, Love your enemies." The Jew was the religious man of antiquity, but in the hands of Scribes and Pharisees his religion had, alas! degenerated into a religion of hatreds. The very type of that religion in Christ's day, its professed orthodoxy, its avowed theology, was the religion of the Pharisee. The high priests of Judaism at that time were Sadducees; but its accredited teachers, its learned theologians, its respected rabbis, its orthodox expounders, they who sat in Moses's seat, they who gave it out as the very function of their lives to detect and exclude heresy, by making an impregnable hedge around God's word,[1] they were the Pharisees. Was *their* religion a religion of compassion? I say that it was a religion of hatred and contempt. They despised women, and held their robes so as not to touch them when they passed; they despised the unlearned, and called them empty cisterns; they despised the poor, and were avaricious and oppressive; they despised the people, who they said knew not the law and were accursed; they hated the Sadducee, because he opposed their influence; they hated the Samaritan, because he did not accept their temple; they hated the Gentiles, and called them dogs; they hated the disciples because they had listened to the voice of truth; they hated the Lord Himself because He rejected their ablutions and scrupulosities, and told them that their loud professions were but the disguise of violence, of corruption, and of self.[2] Do you wonder that Christ said again and again

---

[1] *Pirke Abhoth*, 1. "Make a hedge around the Law."

[2] Those only who are entirely ignorant of the subject will say that one single expression in this passage is exaggerated. It would be easy to refer to whole pages of the Gospels, and to

to these professors and theologians, "Woe unto you, Scribes and Pharisees, hypocrites!" What is it but hypocrisy when little remains to mark the religious man but an intense spite against those who cannot accept his shibboleths; an exceptional bitterness in blackening and persecuting those who, in some outlying question, differ from himself? But woe to that religion, aye, all woes of the Mountain of Beatitudes, to that religion which, however dominant it may seem, has degenerated into a religion of hatreds. It is salt that has lost its savour. It is neither fit for the land nor yet for the dunghill. It is fit only to be trampled under foot.

And if the world in Christ's day needed the lesson of compassion, does the world less need it now? Is there among us no cruel selfishness of pleasure? no cruel luxury of riches? Is there no cruel gratification of passion, pitilessly ignoring the anguish of its

---

scores of passages in the *Talmud* in proof of every sentence. Some illustration may be found in my *Life of Christ*, vol. i. pp. 440—448; ii. 471—478.

victims? No cruel pursuit of gain, recklessly indifferent to the ruin of its dupes? And have priests and theologians never degraded Christianity also into a religion of hatreds? Answer even now the tone of their so-called religious controversy, with its glaring injustice, its fierce innuendoes, its acrid jealousies, its unblushing falsehoods. Answer that "theological hatred," which has passed into a proverb for the most implacable of hatreds. Answer page on page, disowned now, but standing there as a witness against them, of exultant, of pitiless description of unutterable torments. Answer, in days not so far removed, the savage persecution of well nigh every great soul which has had new truths to utter, or old truths to call forth from oblivion. Answer the cords wherewith it has strangled, the rocks down which it has hurled, the fires in which it has choked out the voice of truth. Oh, as the corruption of the best is ever the worst, so has the corruption of religion in the hands of many of its votaries been the pregnant curse of mankind. And though the mode of persecution is altered, though God's unrecognised prophets have wrung from reluctant Pharisees the unwilling boon of liberty and toleration, the world still needs to learn—the so-called "religious" world needs most of all to learn—the meaning of the fact that the denunciation of the Saviour fell on one class, and one alone; and that not on the erring and the ignorant; not on publicans or harlots; not on Samaritans or even Sadducees; but on the one class of hard, anathematising Pharisees, the class which can be most briefly described as that of loveless religionists. We profess and call ourselves Christians; have we yet learnt the simplest and earliest element in the sigh of the Saviour, the divineness of mercy, of compassion, and of love?

2. Yet we must learn the lesson not of compassion only, but of *energy* therewith. Compassion which ends in compassion may be nothing more than the luxury of egotism; but the sigh of Jesus was but an instant's

episode in a life of toil. If His sigh binds us to pity all sin and all sorrow, it binds us no less to bend every effort of our lives towards the end that sin may cease and be forgiven, and sorrow flee away.

For instance, the world lieth in Heathendom. Seven hundred millions of the human race know not the true God, and have not called upon His name. The sigh of Christ pledges us to send to them or to carry to them the witness of His Gospel, to tell them the glad tidings of His salvation.

The world is liable to terrible calamities. The sigh of Christ pledges us to learn the secrets, to obey the laws which may avert or diminish them; to do our utmost by wise care, and enlightened understanding, and faithful self-government to lessen to the utmost of our power every remediable misery of mankind.

The world is full of sorrow. The sigh of Christ pledges us as our first duty not to add to that sorrow, either actively or passively, either directly or indirectly, by our pride or self-indulgence, by cruelty or malice, for our gain or our gratification, by taking unfair advantages, or by speaking false and bitter and unwholesome words.

The world is full of disease. The sigh of Christ pledges us not only to be gentle, and sympathetic, and helpful to all who are afflicted, but also to strive by pureness and kindness, by high example and sound knowledge, to improve the conditions which shall make life sweet and healthy, cheerful and genial, vigorous and pure. It pledges us by every means in our power to find for ourselves and for others the blessed secrets of a sound body in temperance, soberness, and chastity; of a sound mind in that setting our affections on things above which is the best remedy for earthly care.

Lastly, the world is full of sin. The sigh of Christ pledges us ourselves to keep innocency and do the thing that is right; to do our utmost to suppress all sins that are nationally preventible; not to set examples which lead to sin; not to disseminate the causes of sin; to lead men, both by our life and doctrine, to that Saviour who died for sin, and who can alone forgive it, and cleanse us from its guilt and power.

And if so, as we have the creed of our faith, ought we not also to have the vow of our practice? and ought it not to run somewhat as follows?—Seeing that God loves us, that He desires our happiness, that He has given us our lives to be spent in His service, that He sent His Son to die for us and to save us;— seeing that this world might be made a far happier place, and life a far more blessed state than it is if men were wise, and pure, and true to each other, or even if they were not to each other the sorest, surest ill,—therefore, for His sake who died for me and pitied me, I too will be compassionate and active for my brother man. I will pray for him as my Saviour prayed, and work for him as my Saviour worked. If he hates me, I will still try to love him. The man who has slandered or injured me, openly or in secret, even him will I meet with frank kindness and entire forgiveness. I will keep my tongue from every species and variety of evil speaking, lying, and slandering. I will neither write nor cause to be written, either with my name or without my name, any unworthy satire, or sneer, or sarcasm, which shall cause needless pain. "I will not deceive nor cause to be deceived, nor hurt nor cause to be hurt, nor rob nor cause to be robbed, any human being for my gain or pleasure."[1] I will be diligent in man's service whether he accept or refuse my efforts, I will believe evil of no one unless I am forced to believe it, and I will put a bad construction on nothing while a good is possible. I will be kind to many, will wish to be kind to all, will do harm consciously to none. I will think and let think. I will bear and forbear. I will forgive even a difference of opinion. I will be ashamed of nothing but sin. I will love, I will honour, I will labour for man my brother,

---

[1] Ruskin, *Fors Clavigera.*

because God loves us who is our Father, and Christ died for us who is the first-born in this great family of man.

3. My brethren, he who lives thus, will not have lived in vain. He may be poor, he may be despised, he may have seen hundreds of weaker men, and worse men, grow rich and successful, and beat him in what is called the race of life; but assuredly he shall find the life which for Christ's sake he seems to have lost. And let no one say, "I am nobody, I know nothing; every one scorns me; what can I do?" Little may be much, my brother. The widow's two farthings were more than the gifts which the rich cast into the treasury. Who knows how much God may increase and multiply our miserable quota towards the stream of human improvement? After all, it is but the dewdrops and the raindrops which go to make the mighty river and the mighty sea. The poor lad took with him but five barley-loaves and two small fishes, and lo! they fed all the hungry multitude! If we do

but save our own soul, if we help to save but one other soul, how precious a work is that! how dear to God! God cares for the individual. He cares for every one of you. It is the characteristic of an immoral tyranny to deal only with men in masses; but no true child of God can merge the individual in the class. Every soul is precious to Him, because every soul is one for which Christ died. There could be no surer proof that the religious life of the Pharisee of every age is a false religious life than that it is ever characterised by a hideous selfishness. The Pharisee said, "Of what consequence are the dogs of the Gentiles?" Christ said, "Go and preach the gospel to every creature." The Pharisee said, "Thank God I am not as the publican." Christ said that the publican went down to his house justified rather than the other. The Pharisee used the name Samaritan as his term of bitterest reproach; Christ chose the Good Samaritan as the type of the highest virtue. The Pharisee said, Moses commanded that "such as she be stoned;" Christ saw in her a soul to be saved, and said to her gently, "Go, and sin no more." Realise but this, that "we are all His offspring;" that it is not His wish that one of us should perish; that if we but help to save one soul we shall have given a fresh joy to the angels in heaven; realise but that one truth, and even that may enable us to escape the average, to arise above impurity, and falsehood, and sordidness into something higher and more heroical, into some share in the sorrow and the joy of Christ.

4. And when I think on all this, when I remember that love is "not so much a virtue as a substratum of all virtues, the virtue of virtue, the goodness of goodness;" when I think that "*God is love;*" when I read that, amid the unnumbered choirs of heaven, each shall retain his individual life, and have a name which none knoweth but himself; when I see the latent germs and possibilities of goodness which exist even in the worst; when I think that a wretched, sinful man is but the marred

clay of some sweet, innocent, and lovely child; when I read how Jesus so loved our race that He left the glory of Heaven to die amid its execration; when the Gospels tell me *Who* it is that searches for the lost sheep until He find it; *Who* wept on the neck of the prodigal, *Who* suffered the harlot to bathe His feet with tears; *Who* prayed for His murderers; *Who* with one look of tenderness broke the heart of His backsliding apostle; *Who* in one flash of forgiveness made of the crucified robber a saint of God:—when the boundless promises of Scripture crowd upon my mind;—when I recall the hymn which we sing—

> " Mine is an unchanging love,
> Higher than the heights above,
> Deeper than the depths beneath,
> True and faithful, strong as death,"—

when I read that God will not forget His people, though the mother may forget her sucking child;—then there come into my mind two thoughts, with which I will conclude.

(*a*) One thought is the thought of *hope for ourselves ;*—the perfect confidence with which each one of us may throw ourselves upon His love ; the infinite conviction with which we may each of us say, "Christ died for *me*." How many of us here present feel and know ourselves to be defeated men ? We have not been good, we have not done good. We are not what we might have been. We are not worthy to live. Our knowledge is ignorance ; our wisdom foolishness ; our very tears want washing. Well, my brethren, then we are the very ones—the Gentiles, the Samaritans, the lost, the outcast, the sinners, the prodigals—whom Christ came to save. And He is *Christus consolator*—Christ the consoler ; Christ the Good Physician ; Christ the Saviour and Healer of the world. Go to Him in confidence, my brethren, for He is tender to pity and strong to save. Go to Him, young man, the slave and victim of evil passions, and ask Him to save you from yourself. Go to Him, guilty and despairing sufferer ; go to Him, careworn toiler; go to Him, sick and weary sinner, since it was exactly for you—for the helpless who feel their helplessness, for the guilty who know their guilt—that Jesus died. His office is to save, ours to look to Him for help. "If passion rises in thee, go to Him as a demoniac. If deadness creeps upon thee, go as a paralytic. If dissipation comes, go as a lunatic. If darkness clouds thy face, go as a Bartimæus. And when thou prayest, go always as a leper, crying as Isaiah did, 'unclean! unclean!'"[1]

(β) And the other thought is one of *hope for all the world.* Who was it that sighed and said, "*Ephphatha,* be opened"? Ah! it takes the fourfold gospel to answer that question. It was He whom St. Matthew set forth as the Divine Messiah who fulfilled the past; and St. Mark as the Son of God, filling with power and awfulness the present; and St. Luke as the Seeker and Saviour, to all ages, of the lost; and St.

[1] Berridge.

John, in the spiritual gospel, as the Incarnate Word. It was

> "*The very God*—think, Abib!—dost thou think?"

My brethren, it is *this* thought that gives me hope. An awful silence hangs over the grave. God's judgments are a great deep. It may be—I for one have never questioned it—that even if there be mercy beyond the grave—it *may* be, I say, that your soul and mine may perish, and perish for ever and ever. Yet if all that men have said be true; if, indeed, the vast majority of mankind be doomed for ever, without an end and without a respite, to inconceivable horrors—then I confess my own utter inability to see how in this the blessed, pitying Saviour could see of the travail of His soul and be satisfied. Answer me before God, answer me in the depths of your consciences, answer me without subterfuge or periphrasis,—which is most like the heart of Jesus, as revealed in the Incarnation and the Cross—the oft-repeated thought of theologians, from the days of Tertullian to those of Jonathan Edwards, that the saints in their blessedness shall gaze unmoved, nay, even with rejoicing, upon the everlasting tortures of the damned, or the cry of the poet :—

> "Is heaven so high
> That pity cannot enter there?
> Its happy eyes for ever dry,
> Its holy lips without a prayer?
> My God, my God, if thither led
> By Thy free grace unmerited,
> No palm or crown be mine, but let me keep
> A heart that still can feel, and eyes that still can weep"?

It may not be the language of the cowering slave, but surely it is the language of the trustful, loving son to our Father in Heaven. Ah my brethren, leave this question out of sight altogether if you will. Let each hold respecting it what he is taught of God. Let each be thoroughly convinced in his own mind. Hard dogma may be forced upon the soul by the terrors of rack and flame; but hope is a lily of the valley which can grow only in the humble hearts where God shall plant it. For myself, while I ever bear in mind who it was who sighed for the sorrow and sin of many, I will not cease to believe that as man's work here is a work of pity and of energy, because it is a work of hope; so it may be permitted us to believe that the work of Christ may be more fruitful and more limitless than many men have taught, and that His Cross may be as everlasting and victorious in its efficacy as it is set forth to be in the language of the great apostle whose conversion to-day we celebrate. The sun shines, my brethren, and we see the things that are near us,—all the little things that flit in the air, or creep beside our feet. The sun sets, and then first we see the unnumbered stars of heaven, repaying to the sun its sunlight, or burning with independent glory through all the unfathomable space. May it not be so with life and death? Life sets; its insect greatnesses cease to buzz about us; its insect littlenesses cease to sting. We lose sight even of this vault of light and blue which is above our heads; but lo! from under the shadow of death the heavens above us seem to burst open to their depths, and we see not one sun, but systems, and constellations, and galaxies, white with the confluent lustre of suns numberless in multitude and indistinguishable from their distance. May not *death* first reveal to us, as night first reveals to us, the undreamt of glories, the possibilities hitherto inconceivable, which crowd the universe of God? And through all that universe our Father reigns,—God, who was in Christ reconciling the world unto Himself. "Whither," says the Psalmist, "shall I go then from Thy spirit; or whither shall I go then from Thy presence? If I climb up into heaven, Thou art there. If I go down into hell, Thou art there also. If I take the wings of the morning and fly into the uttermost parts of the sea, even there also Thy hand shall lead me, and Thy right hand shall hold me." Yes, my brethren, *God is everywhere;* and the footsteps of Him who sighed for the miseries of man have illuminated even that unknown land which every man must enter. Which of us then would not breathe that bold and trustful prayer of the ancient Rabbi, as he entered the Holy of Holies to burn incense and thought that he saw before him Acathriel, the Crown of Glory, the vision of the Most High—"May it please Thee to let Thy compassion subdue Thine anger. May it be revealed above Thine other attributes, and mayest Thou deal with Thy children according to Thy mercy, and not according to the strict measure of Thy justice"?[1] And offering that prayer, which of us will not believe, that to us, as to the Rabbi in the Vision, the Lord will bow His head to us, as though pleased therewith? I for one believe that with such a prayer, "that it would please Him to have mercy upon *all men*," He is not displeased;— and that is why

> "I walk with bare hushed feet the ground
> Ye tread with boldness shod;
> I dare not fix with mete and bound
> The love and power of God.

---

[1] Berachoth, f. 7, 1

"I know not where His islands lift
    Their fronded palms in air;
I only know I cannot drift
    Beyond His love and care.

"And Thou, O Lord, by whom are seen
    All creatures as they be,
Forgive me if too close I lean
    My human heart on Thee."

SERMON VIII.
LEGISLATIVE DUTIES.

SERMON VIII.

LEGISLATIVE DUTIES.[1]

1 Tim. ii. 1, 2.

"*I exhort therefore, that, first of all, supplications, prayers, intercessions, and giving of thanks, be made for all men; for kings, and for all that are in authority; that we may lead a quiet and peaceable life in all godliness and honesty.*"

You have just heard, my brethren, that ancient bidding prayer, which reminds us that the Parliament of England has been, once more, summoned to meet for a special session. It reminds us also that, by a privilege 300 years old, this Church is known as the Church of the House of Commons.[2] Here, in former days, the members

---

[1] A Sermon preached at St. Margaret's, Westminster, at the opening of Parliament, 1879.

[2] In 1734 Parliament granted 3,500*l.* to the Church because it was "as it were a National Church for the use of the House of Commons."

of the House met, year after year, on Ash Wednesday,[1] to hear the exhortations of the greatest divines of the English Church. This parish of St. Margaret's was then the parish of the rich; the church was the church of royalty,[1] and every Sunday the Members of Parliament worshipped here in hundreds. All these conditions are changed. Streets are now abandoned, which were then full of wealthy and noble residents, and the parish is almost exclusively a parish of the poor. But the church has its memories. We are met within the same walls which were thronged by the Commons of England during the stormiest epochs of their career.[2] Pym,

---

[1] Volumes of these "Fast Day Sermons" are still extant, as Mr. Carlyle says, in rows of "dumpy quartos." Among those who thus preached before the House of Commons at St. Margaret's are Latimer, Usher, Tenison, Tillotson, Gauden, Sherlock, Stillingfleet, Porteus, Baxter, Spratt, Burnet, Atterbury, Horne, Dr. Young, &c.

[2] The royal pews are seen in old pictures of the church. In St. Margaret's Church, on September 25th, 1642, both Houses of Parliament swore to the Solemn League and Covenant with the Assembly of Divines and the Scottish Commissioners. On May 31, 1642, the news of Waller's plot was

and Hampden, and Vane, and Eliot, and Marvell, and Harrington have here knelt in prayer no less than Strafford, and Falkland, and Prince Rupert;[1] and the altar and the font are associated with the memories alike of Milton, the secretary of Cromwell, and Clarendon, the historian of Charles, and Sir William Waller, the Parliamentary general.[2] But apart from all these constitutional associations, the mere fact that

whispered to Pym as he was worshipping in this church on a fast day.

[1] The following are one or two of the remarkable entries in the Chuchwardens' Accounts of the 17th century :—

1627. Paid for bread and wine, when the Rt. Hon. the Commons House of Parliament, being 468 persons, received the Communion in the Parish Church, 1626, 5*l*. 7*s*.

1628. Paid to the ringers, when His Majesty granted the Petition of Right, 5*s*.

1648. Laid out in expenses, when we by order sent forth scouts to bring intelligence of the armies' approach toward the Citie, 12*s*. 6*d*.

1677. To the ringers, on the day when the Prince of Orange was contracted to the Lady Mary, 10*s*.

[2] The following are a few out of many interesting entries in the Parish Register :—

1627. Henry Hide, now Earle of Clarendon, son to Edward, Lord Chancellor and Earle of Clarendon, baptised.

Parliament has again assembled might well furnish the subject for our morning exhortation; and since we cannot but feel in that event a special interest, I purpose this morning to break for one Sunday the course which I had begun, and to ask you to dwell with me for a few moments on the thoughts which a new Session of Parliament suggests. I need not say that they will be religious thoughts. The functions of a pastor are not the same as those of a citizen, and the occasions are rare (and this is not one of them) in which it could be the duty

---

1631, July 5. [Married.] Edmund Waller to Ann Backer.

1656. [Banns.] John Milton, of this parish, Esq., and Mrs. Katherin Woodcock, of the parish of Aldermanbury, spinster. Published October 22, 27, November 3.

1657, October 19. [Baptism.] Katherin Milton, D. to John, Esq., by Katherin. (Underneath this entry some one has written, "This is Milton, Oliver's secretary.")

1657, February 10. [Burials.] Mrs. Katherin Milton. (This is Milton's second wife, to whom he addresses the 23rd Sonnet.)

1657, March 20. Mrs. Katherin Milton. (This is Milton's infant child.)

1668, October 6. Sir William Waller, Knt.

1693, March 14th. Thomas, son to Gilbert Burnett, Lord Bishop of Sarum, baptised.

of the preacher to deal polemically with those burning questions which awaken the animosities of party strife. No! it is his duty, and a blessed one it is, to deal with those indestructible principles which are, to the transient questions of political division, as is the ocean to its wreaths of foam; with those truths which tower above all passing questions, and lie behind them, wide as eternity and deep as life. It is his duty to enforce the deep moral obligations of Christian citizenship, not to thrust himself needlessly into the arena of its evanescent strifes. It is his duty to plead for mutual appreciation; to soften bitternesses; to dwell on points of agreement; to urge that generosity is nobler than violence, that courtesy is more honourable than invective; to bear witness—even to statesmen in the heat of controversy—that

> "One small touch of charity
> Would raise them nearer godlike state,
> Than if the crowded orb should cry
> As those who cried 'Diana great.'"

Times indeed there have been, and may be again, when at all costs the Christian preacher must cry aloud and spare not; times, like those described in the first lesson of the service, when the laws of God have been imperilled; when the principles of justice have been traversed; when the rights of the many have been crushed under the encroachments of the few; when wealth and power have tyrannously pressed their privileges, and forgotten utterly their duties; when men have called evil good, and good evil; put bitter for sweet, and sweet for bitter. At such times the Christian preacher should, like the ancient prophets, speak out, even before kings, and not be ashamed. But my duties to-day are wholly different. I wish to make our bidding prayer, which we use every Sunday during the session of Parliament, real to you; I wish to impress on you the grandeur and solemnity of the functions of our legislature, and to urge upon you the duty of not forgetting as you kneel at the throne of grace those on whom rest such grave responsibilities.

2. "I exhort," says St. Paul, "that supplications, prayers, intercessions, and giving of thanks

be made for all men." It is a grand and elevating duty. "But thou," says the dying king in the *Idylls*,—

> "If thou shouldst never see my face again,
> Pray for my soul; more things are wrought by prayer
> Than this world dreams of. Therefore let thy voice
> Rise like a fountain for me, night and day.
> For what are men better than sheep or goats,
> That nourish a blind life within the brain,
> If, knowing God, they lift not hands of prayer
> Both for themselves and those who call them friend?
> For so the whole round world is every way
> Bound by gold chains about the feet of God."

But the Apostle proceeds especially to urge prayers "for kings and all in authority, that we may lead a quiet and peaceable life in godliness and honesty." Nor have Christians ever overlooked this injunction. In the very earliest liturgies we find prayers for rulers. "With outspread hands," says Tertullian, "we pray for all sovereigns a long life, a secure dominion, a safe home, brave armies, a faithful senate, an upright people, a quiet world."[1] Now in England the strongest power is that of the

---

[1] See Tert. *Apol.* c. 30, 32; *Ad. Scap.* 2.

Parliament. It results from the entire growth of our constitution, that the authority of Parliament, which is ultimately the will of the people, is irresistible and supreme. Even the Plantagenets felt that force, and it wrung from them the strongest charters of our liberty. Even the Tudors felt it, and it curbed their lion will. In vain did the Stuarts fight against it. When James I., on receiving a deputation from the House, ordered so many gilded chairs to be set, "for," he said, "there are so many kings a-coming," he did but utter an unconscious prophecy of a force which was to cost his son a life, and his family a throne. And since then the Parliament of England has been the mainstay of England's liberties; its will has been the motive force, its laws the sheet-anchor of the state. Thank God we all love and honour the Crown of England with a most loyal affection, and we rejoice that there is a House of Lords, lifted above the perils of immediate unpopularity, representing the most established rights and recruited yearly by the noblest intellects;

and yet, again and again, the towering fasces of the sovereign, and of the aristocracy have been loyally and fitly lowered before the majesty of a people's will. And if this be the grandeur of a senator's position, it is the privilege of ours. The members of the House of Commons are not our tyrants, but our representatives; not our masters, but the agents of our will. We are a people, and it is through them that we speak in a people's voice. For these blessings of freedom and self-government we ought to thank God. Citizens, by this gift, of no mean commonwealth, we ought not, amid the dwarfing selfishness of individualism, to forget that, in the formation of that enlightened public opinion by which the issues of legislation are decided, it is our duty to take a part which, however humble, ought to be both thoughtful and sincere. And the slow, just, legal growth of this glorious prerogative is the great characteristic of English history. Even our civil wars, stained as they were with a king's blood, had none of those lurid scenes of riot, those hideous excesses of revolution, which have reddened page after page of the annals of France, and caused her fortunes to oscillate with such terrible violence between the extremes of anarchy and despotism. There is not an Englishman among us all who ought not to feel and to rejoice that he is a son of

> "The land which freemen till,
>   Which sober-suited Freedom chose,
>   A land, where, girt with friends or foes,
>   A man may speak the thing he will;
>
> "A land of settled government,
>   A land of free and old renown,
>   Where freedom slowly broadens down
>   From precedent to precedent."

We then—more perhaps than any nation under the sun—owe this debt of "thanksgiving" to God, of which the Apostle reminds us, "for kings, and all who are in authority."

3. And if we have such large reason to offer those thanksgivings, may not this be due, in no small degree, to the "prayers and supplications" which St. Paul tells us that we ought also to offer? All that there is among us of peace, of progress, of prosperity is due to the collective

wisdom of the nation, as guided by the voice of her Parliament ; and if that wisdom have produced rich results, must we not believe that God has heard the prayers of His people? If "every good gift, and every perfect gift," to nations as well as to individuals, is from above, must it not be due to His goodness that so many statesmen have been raised up among us whose great example is the heritage of the world? Ought we not to thank God for these great men,—for their learning, for their dignity, for their eloquence, for their inflexible determination, to the utmost of their power, to be just and fear not? I will not go too far back. I will not evoke from their marble silence the stately figures of the great Royalists and the great Puritans ; but even in the last generations ought we not to thank God for having raised up such men among us as Chatham and Mansfield, as Burke and Fox, as Pitt and Wilberforce, as Peel and Canning, as Wellington and Russell? They erred, doubtless, each and all of them, as we all err, but for the most part they erred only with honour, and from human limitations; and the shadow of their mistakes has been lost in the splendour of their services. And what treasuries have they left us of immortal truths, clothed in immortal language! what echoes of their mighty voices come rolling to us through the years! "I will do my duty unawed. What am I to fear? That *mendax infamia* from the press which daily coins false facts and false motives? The lies of calumny carry no terror for me. I trust that the temper of my mind, and the colour and conduct of my life have given me a suit of armour against these arrows."—"I wish popularity, but it is that popularity which follows, not which is run after. It is that popularity which never fails, sooner or later, to do justice to the pursuit of noble ends by noble means. I will not do that which my conscience tells me is wrong to gain the applause of thousands, or the daily praise of all the papers that come from the press. I will not avoid doing that which my conscience tells me is right, though it should draw on me the whole artillery of libels, all that falsehood and malice can invent, or the credulity of a deluded populace can swallow."[1] What good man may not be cheered to pursue the fearless path of duty by those strong words of the great Lord Mansfield? What Englishman does not feel how national error should be repudiated when he hears the glorious cataract of eloquence in which Chatham called on the House of Lords to examine, thoroughly and decisively, an inhuman measure, and "to stamp upon it an indelible stigma of the public abhorrence?"[2] Who is not inspirited in the cause of humanity as he reads the glowing and immortal eulogy pronounced by Edmund Burke upon John Howard, the angel of the prisons? Who is not encouraged to hope, even against hope, in the struggle against mighty interests enlisted with national custom in the cause of ruin, when

---

[1] Speech of Lord Mansfield, when surrounded by a mob in the Court of the King's Bench, on a trial respecting the outlawry of John Wilkes, June 8, 1768.   [2] November 18, 1777.

he sees how for twenty years, through good report and evil report, William Wilberforce fought the battle of the slave? Who may not gain from contemplating the indomitable courage of Castlereagh and the stainless integrity of Pitt? Who does not recognise the wisdom and the nobleness of acknowledging an intellectual error when he reads how, for the good of his country, Peel changed his mind? In whose eyes does not a life of duty in the public service—sometimes it may be wanting in insight, but never lacking in inflexible faithfulness—become more noble when he thinks of Wellington as we used to see him, "like some silver-headed eagle of the gods, grown grey in service"? Who is not strengthened to believe in the cause of progress and liberty as he lingers over the long and brave career of John, Earl Russell? Ennobled by the large aims and generous services of these great men, and such as these, amid our general prayers and more special supplications, ought we not also to thank God for England, that

> "Statesmen in her councils met,
> Who knew the season when to take
> Occasion by the hand, and make
> The bounds of freedom broader yet,
> By shaping some august decree,
> Which kept her throne unshaken still,
> Firm based upon her people's will,
> And compassed by the inviolate sea"?

4. And let none of us, my brethren, be so vulgarly absorbed by our shops and our families, by our private interests and selfish domesticities, as to think that Parliaments and laws make small difference to him. Their functions are so far-reaching that there is not a home or hearth in England which is not happier or more dismal from their influence. Not only does the safety of nations, the peace of churches, the prosperity of commerce depend on them, but even no little of the security, the order, the happiness of our individual lives. With them rests the continuance of the loyal affection of our colonies, over realms on which the sun

never sets. To them we owe it that the shores

> "Of Australasia, lustrated at length,
> Collect no longer the putrescent weed
> Of Europe, flung by senates to infect
> The only unpolluted continent."[1]

When some great social iniquity has entrenched itself in the citadels of power it is theirs to drive the battering-ram against its walls. If men, in greed or ignorance, have infected the sweet rivers of England with filthy stains—if they have neglected the laws of nature by perpetuating the conditions of disease—if they have made cities unhealthy by poisoning the air with sulphurous chemicals and the soil with the relics of the dead—if individual selfishness has ever tried to encroach, in a thousand directions, on universal rights;—if deadly poisons are sold with ruinous facility;—if national sins are perpetuated by the reckless diffusion of

---

[1] W. S. Landor's lines to Mrs. Chisholm. The Abolition of Transportation was proposed by Archbishop Whately and Sir W. Molesworth in 1846, and by Lord Cranworth in 1853. It was finally carried out in 1857 under Sir G. Grey's Act.

terrible temptations; — if scoundrels would deprave with pestilent literature the morals of our sons;—if landlords will crowd the poor into tenements scarce fit for swine; — if banded unions have striven to persecute opinion and make thought a crime—then theirs is the godlike function to secure dwellings for the honest; to shield the innocence of the young; to diminish the perils of the tempted; to repress the violences of the criminal; to protect the independence of the thinker; to prevent the recklessness of the avaricious; to see that none grow rich on profits drawn from the nation's ruin; to restore its crystal to the river, and its sweetness to the air;—by fearless repression of wrong, by wide encouragement of right, by high moral influence, by strong sanitary legislation, it is theirs to secure the righteousness of our land, and the health of our people. The sundial of Lincoln's Inn says, "*Lex anchora Regni*,"—Law, the anchor of the realm; and since the majestic principle of that Divine Law, "whose home is the bosom of God and her voice the harmony of the world," can only be ensured by human laws, it is the function of Parliaments, in the words of a recent statesman, to be able to claim that 'they found law dear and left it cheap; they found it a sealed book, they left it an open letter; they found it the patrimony of the rich, they left it the inheritance of the poor; they found it the two-edged sword of craft and oppression, they left it the staff of honesty and the shield of innocence.'[1] Only the future will be able duly to estimate the full beneficence of the home legislation of the last fifty years. Take but the abolition of the Test Acts, with their tyrannies and hypocrisies, in 1828. Take the abolition of slavery in 1830. Take the Reciprocity of duties, which so vastly increased our shipping in 1829. Take the Reform Bill, which saved the very bases of our constitution in 1832. Take the abolition of the Corn Laws, with the vast relief which it gave to a teeming

---

[1] See speech of Lord Brougham in the House of Commons on *Law Reform*, Feb. 7, 1828.

population, in 1846. Take the Bill for the protection of women and children in mines and colleries in 1842.¹ Take the shortening of the weary hours of factory labour in 1847. Take the large measure for the purification of the Thames in 1858. Take the establishment of a national system of education in 1870. Take the Acts for the protection of life and property in mines, and railroads, and ships, and banks, and companies. Take the defence of even dumb animals from reckless cruelty, and the preservation of the harmless birds of land and wave. There is not one man of us all in England who has not gained by the blessings which flow from measures such as these; and it is due in no small degree to them that population is nearly doubled; wealth vastly increased; crime diminished; longevity extended; our Empire vaster; our people stronger; classes more united; Englishmen better governed, better taught, better housed, better protected, and

¹ See Molesworth's *History of England* from 1830. i. 323; ii. 109, &c.

better fed. And how is it, that—often in the very teeth of the most determined and unscrupulous opposition,—these triumphs have been won? Chiefly because God has given us statesmen with the insight to perceive their blessedness, and the courage to enforce their necessity, and Parliaments with whom reason has been stronger than prejudice, and opponents ready to acquiesce with loyalty even in those measures which have subordinated private interests to the public good. When they have passed peacefully into law, victorious over passionate antagonism, men have felt gladly that a great strain was removed. Some here are old enough to remember the passing of the Great Reform Bill in 1832. Passions were then so intensely excited, that, in another country, a throne might well have toppled over into the dust; and even in our own country it seemed at one time as if Revolution sat 'nursing the impatient earthquake.' And yet, by God's blessing, all was done by legal and constitutional processes. A great man who was present at one of the final divisions has told us that it was a scene never to be forgotten,—like seeing Cæsar stabbed in the senate-house, or Cromwell ordering the removal of the mace. From the 608 members present, the Ayes and Noes came like volleys of artillery; with breathless silence the votes were counted; suppressed cries began to break out towards the close, and when it was known that there was a narrow majority of eight in favour of the bill, strong men burst into weeping and laughter, and the stillness of the night was broken by storms of loud huzzahs, which swept far along the dark excited streets.[1]

5. I have tried, then, to show you why, as English citizens, it is a plain duty for us, as we do, to pray for the Parliament which thus powerfully sways our social legislation. You will be well aware that issues even vaster—issues affecting other nations no less than our own, hang upon our foreign policy. I am not one

---

[1] See a letter in Mr. Trevelyan's *Life of Lord Macaulay*, i. 205. See, too, Miss Martineau's *History*, ii. 58—71.

of those who hold that war is of necessity a crime. In a corrupt and guilty world it may be as necessary as the storm is necessary to cleanse the pestilence from the stagnant air; and I doubt whether even the Apostle of Love himself would have denied that there are crises at which we are forced to use even the tremendous words of the most Christian and gentle-hearted of poets, that

> "God's most perfect instrument
> For carrying out a pure intent,
> Is men arrayed for mutual slaughter,
> Yea, carnage is His daughter."

But though there are such awful crises, I am sure that every one of us as Christians feels how grave is the responsibility of deciding, *when* it is expedient, when it is necessary,—yea, lawful, yea, right,—to stretch forth our hands for that sword of justice, which is of celestial temper, and forged in the armoury of God. For the disinterestedness of our justice, do we not all know how strict and solemn an account statesmen as statesmen, and we as citizens must one day give at the judgment-seat of God? Do we not feel that to all who in the awful impartial eyes of God fight without this solemn sense of responsibility a voice falls from heaven, "Put up again thy sword into his place, for all they that take the sword shall perish with the sword"? My brethren, it is not of course in any way my wish, either directly or indirectly, to express an irresponsible private opinion upon a burning question; but it is my wish that we should all alike be reminded of the duty of praying for those who, as in God's sight, are called on to decide these awful issues. They, be sure, even when they deem war necessary, feel to the full as keenly as we can do that war is dreadful; they with all of us look back to that Christian principle of arbitration six years ago, when we, "an old and haughty nation proud in arms," bowed nobly to a decision which judged us to be wrong, and thereby had the inestimable reward of having changed bitter differences into hearty friendship. And all of us alike, I am very sure, look forward to the happier day, when, in a just and faithful world, the war-drum shall throb no longer,

> "And the battle-flags be furled
> In the Parliament of man, the federation of the world."

6. These then, my brethren, are the reasons why, in this Church of the House of Commons, we pray "for the Great Council of the nation now assembled in Parliament." May we feel, as often as we hear that bidding prayer, how real it is. May we recognise that under every form of human government the Lord God is still our King. May our senators have wisdom to realise the grandeur of their duties! May they hand on, unquenched, that torch of freedom which, across the dust and darkness of many centuries, has been handed on to them. May they preserve unimpaired the high prestige and dignity and honour which are their illustrious heritage. May they refer every question to the Law of Righteousness, as read by the light of conscience,—never giving up to party what

was meant for mankind, or to a province what is the heritage of a kingdom, or to a section what is the prerogative of a race;—never forgetting that each vote of theirs will tend, in its measure, to make England a greater and better, or a weaker and poorer land; always on their knees asking God that they may use the power intrusted to them, not for private interests, not for transient ambitions, not for factious triumphs, but always with sternest integrity, and in His faith and fear. So shall we be able to hold our own against every force which can be brought against us; so shall we realise more and more the Psalmist's golden picture of national prosperity, that "truth shall flourish out of the earth, and righteousness look down from heaven. Yea, the Lord shall show lovingkindness, and our land shall give her increase. Righteousness shall go before Him, and He shall direct her going in the way."

SERMON IX.

THE AIMS OF CHRISTIAN STATESMANSHIP.

SERMON IX.

THE AIMS OF CHRISTIAN STATESMANSHIP.[1]

DEUT. XXVIII. 1.

"*And it shall come to pass, if thou shalt hearken diligently to the voice of the Lord thy God . . . . that the Lord thy God will set thee on high above all nations of the earth.*"

THOSE who worship here will, I think, have recognized my desire that, amid the daily endeavour to work out our own salvation with fear and trembling, we should not forget our national duties, our duties as human beings in the great family of man. We suffer even in our spiritual life when we confine our thoughts to the narrow horizon of our individual welfare. If the great remedy for selfishness be to lose ourselves in God, if the great example of

[1] Preached in St. Margaret's, Westminster, Feb. 8, 1880.

unselfishness be the example of Christ, if the great work of Christ was to sacrifice Himself for the sins of the whole world, then surely he must be the best and truest man whose hopes and fears are not wholly absorbed into the silence and seclusion of his interior life, but who yearns for the religion of active service, who desires to follow in the Divine footsteps of Him who "went about doing good." But he who would live thus, while he strives to be a child of God, must never forget that he will be a better child of God in proportion as the whole influence of his life, whether in a large sphere or in a small, tends not to poison but to purify the current of the world's life. If at the words, "I am a man; and therefore in all things human I have a concern," the whole audience of a heathen theatre could rise up to shout their approval, ought not a Christian congregation to feel that those lessons are deeply religious which turn their thoughts to our own work in a Christian nation, and to the work of a Christian nation in the world? It is a mistake to suppose that such questions are too vast and vague. Results the most vast are brought about by the aggregate of small separate exertions. The coral insect is a small and ephemeral creature with soft and feeble body, yet the result of its insignificant existence, the contribution of its tiny grain, rears the leaguelong reef which forms a barrier in the ocean, or builds the bases of continents which form for untold ages the home of man. Let none of us try to prove that we have but little responsibility. "We never die; we are the waves of the ocean of life, communicating motion to the expanse before us, and leaving the history we have made on the shore behind."

2. And if any congregation may ignore the questions which affect our public and corporate usefulness, we cannot. This Church, as I have said before, has at least its memories. It is still, in name, the Church of the House of Commons. Here on every Ash Wednesday, and on every great occasion of national joy or national humiliation, in old

days the whole House of Commons used to come to worship; and here they have been addressed century after century by almost all the great divines of the Church of England from Archbishop Usher down to the close of the Crimean War, when the thanksgiving sermon was preached by Canon Melville.[1] And therefore I shall venture once more to-day to speak of subjects which might be called political. Two days ago most of us witnessed the long and gorgeous procession in which this Parliament was opened by a Queen of England, more beloved than any one of the long line of her royal ancestors. Who, as he gazed on that scene, could fail to indulge in some thoughts of pride and gratitude? Such pride is natural. The slow course of English history, rich in great deeds, and great sacrifices, has made us the inheritors of blessings which if they are awful in responsibility are unexampled in splendour. Look at our Empire. In its extent,

---

[1] See Note on p. 262.

on which the sun never sets, in the consolidation which bows the heart of its peoples like the heart of one man—not the colossal Empires of the East, not the wide realms of Alexander or of the Cæsars can for a moment compare with it. And yet the vastness of our Empire would only be an element of decay and weakness without its solidarity. Were it an Empire of opposed nationalities, only cramped together by an iron tyranny, it would be a thing to blush for, not to be proud of; but thank God it is a loyal Empire, and its colonies not only willingly but gladly kindle the lamps of their Prytaneums from the sacred fire which burns on the altar of their old home. It is an Empire free as England is free, whose soil emancipates the slave who treads on it; and contented as England is contented, where there are no deadly antipathies between the ruled and the ruling, between rich and poor. How can I better sum up points on which I can but touch than in the words of the poet?—

"A people's voice! we are a people yet,
  Tho' all men else their nobler dreams forget,
  Confused by brainless mobs and lawless powers;
  Thank Him who isled us here, and roughly set
  His Briton in blown seas and storming showers,
  We have a voice with which to pay the debt
  Of boundless love, and reverence, and regret,
  To those great men who fought and kept it ours.
  And keep it ours, O God, from brute control.
  O statesmen, guard us, guard the eye, the soul
  Of Europe, keep our noble England whole,
  And save the one true seed of freedom sown
  Betwixt a people and their ancient throne . . .
  For saving that ye help to save mankind.'

I shall speak to you then this morning of matters political; but not, I need scarcely say, of any party politics. You know me I trust too well to think that I should desecrate this pulpit,—from which so many men incomparably wiser and better than myself have spoken—for the seizure of unfair advantages or the inflammation of party animosities. I shall touch only on those eternal principles of which it is well for us at all times to be reminded, but on which all good men of every party ought to be unanimous, however much they may be led to differ as to their applications. And if you ask me how I can venture to speak of politics in the presence of statesmen and senators, I answer that there can be no presumption in the herald who in any presence, however august, does but deliver the message of the King of kings. "Thou," says the priest in one of our dramas, to the British Prince,—

> "Thou art a king, a sovereign o'er frail men,
> I am a Druid, servant of the gods;
> Such service is above such sovereignty."

"Who are you that presume to school the nobles and sovereign of this realm?" asked Mary, Queen of Scots, of John Knox. "Madam," he replied, "a subject born within the same." It would be fatal to England if such principles as I shall touch upon were the monoply of one or of the other party. They tower far above all party questions; they are derived from the eternal laws of God. "For not now or yesterday," as the ancient poet sings, "do these live, but at all times and ever, and no man knows since when they sprang to light."[1] These are "those lofty laws which had their birth in the expanse of heaven, of which God is the sole Father; man begat them not, nor shall oblivion lull them into slumber."[2] There is not one true or righteous earthly law which does not derive its origin from these, even as the great rivers of India have their sources amid the Himalayan snows.

3. There are two great regions of the political action of every state—Foreign and Domestic. By what principles then should every Christian desire them to be directed? In dealing with them what thoughts should every good man desire to be for ever before his eyes?

Let me speak first of what should be the Foreign Policy of England, and let me indulge for a moment in a large retrospect.

You heard in the first lesson of this morning about the three sons of Noah. When first the

---

[1] οὐ γάρ τι νῦν γε κἀχθές, ἀλλ' ἀεί ποτε ζῇ ταῦτα κοὐδεὶς οἶδεν ἐξ ὅτου 'φάνη.—Soph. *Ant.* 455.
[2] Soph. *Œd. Tyr.* 865—871.

separate races of mankind begin to be descernible in the confused sea of humanity, we see dark-skinned and savage tribes living for the most part in the deepest night of barbarism, identified theoretically with the race of Ham. Out of this æon of unprogressive barbarism emerge, in course of time, the great semi-civilised nations of Eastern Asia and Northern Africa, the Chinese and the Egyptians, with their oppressive despotisms and cruel superstitions. Then in the third great æon of human records, from 2,000 to 3,000 years before the birth of Christ, we witness the first definite appearance of those two mighty races, the Semitic and the Aryan, which many have regarded as the race of Shem and the race of Japhet. Fairer in complexion, stronger, more physically beautiful, more intellectually gifted, they appear first in the great table lands of Central Asia, and to them is due almost all that is progressive or noble in the history of mankind. To the Semitic race, and preeminently to the Jew, God entrusted the religious education of the ancient world. To this race it was mainly given to keep alive in the world a belief in the Unity of God, and the Eternal Majesty of the moral law. To the Aryan race, to which we belong, was entrusted mainly the civilisation of mankind; from it sprang mainly the arts of war and peace; the glory that was Greece belongs to it, and the grandeur that was Rome; it has been the parent of the lofty spiritualism of India, the deep philosophy of Germany, the glorious art of Italy, the dauntless energy of England. But its destiny did not culminate until in the crucifixion of our Lord, the Semitic race, knowing not the day of its visitation, proved false to its function and its heritage. Then the torch of the Christian Revelation, which would have been extinguished for ever in the hands of the Semite, was transferred into the hands of the race of Japhet, and soon burst into a lustre which was intended to illuminate the world. Of all the families of that Aryan race we, the English of to-day, have the grandest history and the most magnificent, yet also the most perilous responsibilities. We have colonised the western world. We are undisputed lords of the great southern continent. Our language is already more widely disseminated than any tongue that was ever spoken by the lips of man. It seems likely to become the almost universal language of the future. Who can exaggerate the immensity of such an influence or the awfulness of such duties? They affect many of us directly, and in many ways. Our sons and daughters go to every quarter of the globe, and such as we are they are, and as are the lessons they have learnt in their English homes so will be the influence which they exercise in the most distant colonies. But a vast proportion of these our national duties are summed up in the words, "the Foreign Policy of England." What then should be the one object of that Foreign Policy? Can there be in the light of Christianity any other answer than this — the intellectual, the moral, the spiritual welfare of mankind? Ought we not to teach to the world the lessons of a superior wisdom, a purer justice, a loftier morality? Ought we not to inscribe on the banner of our progress that sacred name which it is at once our highest mission and our most blessed privilege to render visible and glorious through a regenerate world? Much by God's blessing we have done; and we may say of our native country,

> "Yea! she hath mighty witnesses, and though
> Her deeds of good have had their ebb and flow,
> She yet awaits in righteous strength sublime
> The calm cool judgment of all after-time."

But, alas! there is another side of the picture. Whole races have disappeared before the advancing conquests of our sons. The footsteps of our countrymen as they have passed across the world have too often been footsteps dyed in blood. Africa has known them as the buyer of the slave. The islands of the Pacific have known them as the stealer of their youth. The aborigines of Tasmania have known them as the exterminators of their race. Wise and eminent laymen often speak of these things more plainly than we timid, conventional clergymen, terrified as we too often are into a decorum which is cowardice, and into a weakness of statement which is a treachery against eternal truth. And in the last week one great writer has not scrupled to say that the broad result of the labours of Europe "for the salvation of the wild tribes of the New World, since the vaunted discovery of it, may be summed up in the stern sentence—death by drunkenness and small-pox."[1] And another great writer, that whereas fifty years ago there were 1,500,000 Hottentots, there are now about 20,000, and the rest have perished by drink and by disease,[2]— by drink and disease which we have introduced. Ah, my brethren, ought we not to have stern searchings of heart as to the way in which we have dealt with these other sheep of Christ, though they be not of this fold— children with us of a common God, heirs with us of a common immortality? Do we

[1] J. Ruskin, *Contemporary Review*, Feb. 1880.
[2] Froude, *Lectures on South Africa*, p. 13.

not owe them an immense reparation, as well as eternal duties? And do we not owe these duties not to them only but to all our brethren whether they belong to our own or to other races of mankind? In two great ways we influence them,—by war, and by commerce. War is sometimes inevitable, but we have seen in our own days in a neighbouring nation the awful Nemesis which falls on those who enter on it "with a light heart"; and from the greatest of living generals—from him who headed the German armies in that struggle—come this very week the words,—that "every war, however successful, is a general calamity," though that desirable conviction can only be produced by a better moral and religious education of the peoples, "which," he adds, "is the work of centuries."[1] War then there must sometimes be; only let us see that as, in carrying out its dreadful arbitrament, our sons have always been heroically gallant, so in

---

[1] From a letter of Count von Moltke to a Saxon peasant

entering into it we all strive to be inflexibly, rigidly, scrupulously just. Every war that is not absolutely indispensable — every war of mere ambition and of wanton aggression—is a sowing of dragon's teeth. Nor let us ever forget that on all that we do—undisturbed by sophistries, unbribed by interest, judging solely by everlasting laws of righteousness—God will exact His strict retribution, and history record her impartial verdict.

And as it is our duty to mediate thus searchingly before God about every War on which we enter, so it is our duty to look well to our Commerce. Because, and in so far as, our commerce has been honest and true, we have held the markets of the world. Adulteration, greed, selfish monopolies would soon lose them. But is there not one branch at least of our foreign commerce which demands imperiously and at once the most solemn attention of every Christian statesman? Let me ask of every conscience here a plain answer to a plain question. Is the opium trade with China—yes or no—what the trade of a Christian nation ought to be? Does it, or does it not involve the utter ruin of the bodies and souls of thousands of the Chinese?[1] If it does, is the fact that it pours six millions into the revenues of India a necessity of our position or an aggravation of our guilt? Necessity, my brethren? God knows nothing of immoral necessities.[2] And shall it be ever said of England,

> "So spake the fiend, and with necessity,
> The tyrant's plea, excused his devilish deeds"?

And if the profits of a pernicious trade be an aggravation of its guilt and of our guilt who share in those profits, do we think that we shall be made a special exception to the

---

[1] These questions are simply asked *as* questions. There can be no doubt that the minds of many in England are uneasy about this trade, and if it be a moral, righteous, or even defensible trade, all that they desire is to understand the grounds on which it may be so regarded.

[2] The words of the Chinese Imperial Commissioner Lin, in a memorial sent to England, are worth preserving—"In the ways of Heaven no partiality exists, and no sanction is given to

incidence of the slow but certain, of the just but inevitable, punishments of Heaven? Or if the trade be as guilty and as indefensible as to the ordinary onlooker it seems to be, shall we nationally gain by the pecuniary profits of a procrastinated repentance? "It is," if I may quote the words, at the utterance of which I once saw a thrill pass through the Parliament of England, "it is against the ordinances of Providence,—it is against the interests of man—that immediate reparation should be possible when long-continued evils have been at work; for one of the main results of misdoing would be removed, if at any moment the consequences of misdoing could be repaired." Will those consequences

injure them for the sake of our own advantage. Not to use opium oneself, and yet to venture on the manufacture and sale of it, and with it to seduce the simple folk of this land, this is to seek one's own livelihood by the exposure of others to death— to seek one's own advantage by other men's injury; such acts are utterly abhorrent to the nature of men, and utterly opposed to the ways of Heaven." See *British Opium Policy*, by F. S. Turner, p. 281.

of misdoing be easier to avert when they have struck deeper roots and spread over a wider area? If this trade be an immoral one — if being immoral we wilfully continue it,—then let us look to it, for evil is before us. Righteousness—you might write it as the epitome of *all* history, upon the first page of *every* history—Righteousness exalteth a nation, but sin is the reproach of any people. If we never go to war save when justice and righteousness require that we should do so;—if our dealings with every other nation, whether weak or strong, whether civilised or savage, be rigidly and chivalrously upright;—if our commerce be not corrupted at the fount by that horrible selfishness which sacrifices nations to its insatiate greed of gain;—then we may expect, and we shall receive a blessing from the God of all nations, for then the one principle of all our foreign policy will be this,—to aim at ever finding our own highest good in the highest good of all mankind.

And if that be the only righteous answer

to the question, what ought to be the one informing idea of our foreign policy, is not the answer as to our domestic policy like to it? Ought not that also to be directed simply and solely with a view to the common good of all? Is there no earnest vigilance necessary to beat back the encroachments of selfishness on the national wellbeing? Do we need no care to prevent the growth and the assertion of vested interests in anything which is the cause of national calamity? Is there no need of the courage which scorns all popularity save that which is bestowed by after ages on good and virtuous actions? Has there been no need, in all ages and in all lands, for legislators to escape the average? to rise above the conventional? to fix their eyes not on the interests of passing combinations, but on the immutable demands of truth and right? Has there never been more than one statesman of whom it might have been written,

"Who meant for the universe, narrowed his mind,
And to party gave up what was meant for mankind?"

Have there been no occasions on which men have been so carried away by gusts of popular excitement, that instead of regarding the odium incurred by righteous dealing as the highest glory, we might well ask of them,

> " Beneath the heroic sun,
> Is there not one
> Whose sinewy wings of choice do fly
> In the fine mountain air of public obloquy ? "

How wide, my brethren, how noble is the sphere of enlightened Christian politics ! What ample scope is there still for men to win a civic wreath as green as that of Chatham or Wilberforce ! To see that the very weakest and humblest be safe under the inviolable protection of equal laws ; to see that by the universal extension of sound learning and religious education a limit be put to brutality and vice ;—to see that there be a national acknowledgment of our allegiance to Him before whom all nations are but as dust in the balance — does this open no sphere of action wide enough for the most soaring ambition ? Have we nothing to do for the laws of health? by controlling the sale of poisonous drugs; by interfering in time to prevent the rapid growths of new vices; by daring — ere it be too late, — ere the neglected opportunity becomes an irreparable curse — to save yet another generation from the curse of drunkenness? Is there nothing to do for our native land to save its green fields from being blackened by the ashes of the furnace; its seas from the exhaustion of their riches; its waving woods from being withered by the noxious gases of the manufacturer; its sweet rivers from being poisoned by influxes of putrescent slime? Is there no improvement to be hoped for in our cities? If *private* magnanimity be among Englishmen well-nigh a dead virtue, is there no need of *public* magnanimity to carry out with imperial munificence the great works which adorn and beautify them? To touch on small matters at our very doors, are there no means to prevent every foreigner and American who visits England from seeing such a scandalous and grimy waste as this churchyard is, at the very centre of our national life, and at the very gates of our grandest cathedral? Is there no power to check the hideousness and indecency of scandalous placards? is nothing to save us from being depressed, for weeks together, with the dense foulness of smoky fogs? And is there nothing to be done in greater matters than these? If there was exaggeration in the tones which told us that in our great cities the poor were often "swept into incestuous heaps, or into dens and caves which are only tombs disquieted," still is there no necessity for the stern beneficence of righteous legislation to demand and to insist that they should not be huddled together in the seething immorality of unwholesome and unhallowed tenements? And is there not need of perpetual interference to protect the helplessness of individual rights? Much, we most thankfully admit — we may before God most humbly plead — much has been done for the boys and girls in our factories; for the peasant children of our fields; for the waifs and strays of our streets; for the suppression of dangerous employments; for the alleviation of unwholesome trades; for the safety of railway passengers; for the rights of those injured by machinery; to save our sons from being passed through the fire to Moloch, and our sailors plunged in the sea to Mammon—much has been done, but there is much more to do. Take but one instance;—we talk of the cruel and vulgar amusements of the ancient Romans; can anything be much more cruel and vulgar than the disgusting sight of young men and young women half-clad shot through the air from a catapult at a height of sixty feet? and can we wonder that while such are the favourite sights demanded by the raw and crude vulgarity of sightseers, three times in the last few weeks these unhappy persons, —who also suffer much in being trained for such wretched spectacles—have met with the painful and shocking accidents which the newspapers record?[1] Talk of encroachments

[1] Since these words were written I have read the following passage, written by the Queen's command to the Mayor of

on individual liberty, these things are encroachments on individual liberty. There is no true liberty but that which consists in loyal obedience to beneficent laws. There is no true liberty in each man being suffered to infringe as he likes upon the liberty of others. There is no true liberty in an exaggerated individualism. A country demoralised by the terrible fascination of multiplied temptation is a country not free, but enslaved by its own worst interests and fettered by its own vilest propensities. Let all *such* freedom be sternly repressed; it

---

Birmingham in 1863:—On July 20 a poor woman, who went by the name of the French Blondin, had been killed by a fall from the tightrope, and the sports of the assembled multitude had been continued as though nothing had occurred. "Her Majesty," so the letter ran, "cannot refrain from making known to you her personal feelings of horror that one of her subjects —a female—*should have been sacrificed to the gratification of the demoralising taste*, unfortunately prevalent, attended with the greatest danger to the performers. Were any proof wanting that such exhibitions are demoralising, I am commanded to remark that it would be at once found in the decision arrived at to continue the festivities, the hilarity, and the sports of the occasion after an event so melancholy." See Molesworth's *History*, iii. 319.

does but film the ulcerous place of slavery; it is the freedom of reckless selfishness, base in its origin and demoralising in its issues.

> "He is a freeman whom the truth makes free,
> And all are slaves besides."

In one last word, then, of all that I have said this is the sum: Let godless philosophy say what it will, let a cold-blooded political economy say what it will, I say that unless all history be a delusion and all Scripture a lie, then "What is morally wrong cannot be politically right." Of our domestic policy I say that the duty of every Government is to make it "difficult to do wrong and easy to do right;" and that "every state's organisation is perverted, perverse, and doomed to ruin, where single individuals, or single classes have the pretension to constitute the broad bases of society." And of our foreign policy I say that our intercourse with all nations whether strong or weak, will be always wrong, and must be ultimately fatal, if it be not based on the principle that international morality has no separate code, but is only a wider application of the Christian ethics. "Mankind," said a great patriot and a great orator, "has but one single aim; it is Mankind itself; and that aim has but one single instrument—Mankind again." "God," said an inspired Apostle, speaking to contemptuous Pagans, "hath made of one blood all nations of men to dwell on all the face of the earth, and hath determined the times before appointed, and the bounds of their habitation; that they should seek the Lord, if haply they might feel after him, and find him, though he be not far from every one of us: for in him we live, and move, and have our being; as certain also of your own poets have said, For we are also his offspring."

SERMON X.
MANY FOLDS: ONE FLOCK.

O merciful God, who hast made all men, and hatest nothing that Thou hast made, nor wouldest the death of a sinner, but rather that he should be converted and live, we beseech Thee graciously to behold this Thy family, for which our Lord Jesus Christ was contented to be betrayed and given up into the hands of wicked men, and to suffer death upon the Cross, who now liveth and reigneth with Thee and the Holy Ghost, world without end. Amen.—*Collects for Good Friday.*

SERMON X.[1]

John x. 16.

"And other sheep I have which are not of this fold: them also I must bring, and they shall hear my voice; and there shall be one flock, one shepherd."

You heard these memorably beautiful words, my brethren, in this morning's Gospel; and many of you will have detected a slight alteration in my reading of the text; our English version has "Other sheep I have which are not of this fold, them also I must bring that they may be all one *fold and* one shepherd." But the two words rendered "fold" are in the Greek different; what our Lord says is that He, as the one, as the

---

[1] Preached in Westminster Abbey on April 27th, 1879.

Good Shepherd, must lead His other sheep not of this fold that they may all be one *flock*, one shepherd. The *folds* may ever be different; the *flock* is always to be one. It is one of the many points in which our English version loses by want of perfect accuracy. That version is as a whole incomparable in its melody and force; it will ever continue to speak to the ear like music, to the heart like a voice that can never be forgotten; but in many points it will gain in perfectness and truth by the revision which it is now receiving, and since it will lose nothing and gain much, we cannot doubt that the forthcoming version will be accepted with the welcome which it deserves.

2. There is an almost inexhaustible depth and wisdom in these words; and it would be well for us, if, instead of our crude theories of a mechanical inspiration—which have been theories fraught in all ages with the pride and intolerance of individuals, with injury to the Church, and with mischief to mankind—it would be well for us, I say, if, instead of this

superstitious exaltation of the letter which killeth, we accustomed ourselves to understand in their full significance—in the spirit which giveth life,—were it but a few of those passages which reveal to us the deep things of God. In this verse, for instance, there lies a truth hidden from men for æons, but now revealed. That truth is the great Idea of Humanity —of the whole race of mankind as gathered up into one under the Federal Headship of its Lord.

3. In this meaning the very word Humanity was unknown to the ancient world. In Greek there is nothing corresponding to it; in Latin, *Humanitas* means kindly nature or "refined culture." The Jew looked on the world as divided into Jews and Gentiles; of which the Jews were the children of the Most Highest, the Gentiles dogs and sinners. The Greeks looked on the world as divided into Greeks and barbarians; of which the Greeks were the lords of the human race, the barbarians were natural enemies and natural slaves. Jew and Greek

and barbarian, alike looked on mankind as divided into men and women; of which women were fit only for ignorance and seclusion, as the chattels of man's pleasure and the servants of his caprice. And what was the consequence of these errors? It was that the ancient world was cursed with a triple curse,—the curse of slavery, the curse of corruption, the curse of endless wars. What had Christianity to say to this state of things? She taught emphatically and for the first time that there is *no* favouritism with God; that God is no respecter of persons; that in God's sight all men are equally guilty, all equally redeemed; that each man is exactly so great as he is in God's sight and no greater; that man is to be honoured simply as man, and not for the honours of his station, or the accidents of his birth; that neither the religious privileges of the Jew, nor the intellectual endowments of the Greeks, made them any dearer to God than any other children in His great family of man. Christianity taught us in the words of St. Peter, to honour all men;[1] and in the words of St. Paul, that in Christ Jesus there is neither circumcision nor uncircumcision; neither Jew nor Greek; neither male nor female; neither barbarian, Scythian, bond nor free; but Christ all and in all.[2] And these great apostles thus taught, because, in the view of our Lord and Master, mankind were indeed as sheep without a shepherd,—scattered by a thousand wolves, and wandering in the dark and cloudy day,—but He is the Good Shepherd, whose work it was to seek for His lost sheep, and bring them back again into His one flock. In the Jewish temple ran a middle wall of partition, on which were stern inscriptions forbidding any Gentile to set foot within it on pain of death; Jesus came to break down that middle wall; to make God's Temple co-extensive with the universe, and its worshippers with all mankind. The Gospel introduced then into the world a new, a glorious, a beneficent conception: the conception of mankind as one great

---

[1] 1 Pet. ii. 17.
[2] 1 Cor. vii. 19; Gal. v. 6, vi. 15; Col. iii. 11.

brotherhood bound together by the law of love; as one great race;—united to the *universe* by natural laws; united to *God* by the common mysteries of creation and redemption; united to all the dead by the continuity, to all the living by the solidarity of life. And the result of this grand conception is a deadening of that mean and narrow selfishness which is the worst curse of our nature; a widening of the horizon of our hopes and aims; a throwing down of ignorance and prejudice; a more cheerful and hearty devotion to our common work on earth, which is the increase of man's happiness by the free development of his spiritual nature. We learn from it that the Christianity of the pure Gospel is essentially social; that it aims at universal amelioration as well as at individual holiness; that from the common mystery of Death, and the common blessings of salvation, should flow an exuberance of kindness, in which the dearest personal interests are recognised as identical with the highest general good. It is thus from God's own word that we learn that love to Him our Father is best shown by love to man our brother; that "No man for himself, every man for all," expresses the very ideal of a Christian society; that "mankind has but one single aim—mankind itself: and that aim but one single instrument—mankind again."

4. My brethren, these truths—all truths—are worse than useless if they be left neglected in the lumber-room of the memory. These sounding generalities do positive harm,—because they act as opiates to the conscience,—if we are unprepared to give them a practical application. But will you look with me a little closer at this great doctrine—that with God there is no favouritism; and that all the races and ranks of men are one in Christ?—and shall we very humbly try to see together whether it suggests no solemn lessons for our daily life?

i. Many folds; one flock; one shepherd. Look at home. What is the first great obvious fact of society which strikes the attention? Is it not the vast difference between rich and poor? It is perfectly true, that one half the world does not know how the other half lives. A book was lately written in France which professed to be a picture of the life of the lowest orders of French society; and doubtless to the revolting realism of the photograph has been due its immense success.[1] It is a book to make the blood run cold; and yet any one, who, in those dim regions where pauperism reaches to the border-land of crime, has seen anything of the life of those classes,—its dirt, its squalor, its disease, its shamelessness, its drunkenness, its blasphemy, its brutality, its awful ignorance, its reckless obliteration of every religious impulse and every moral law,—knows how much there is of frightful truth in that dark picture. What others think I know not, as to the fate and future of these the too often worse than savages of a nominal Christianity; but, in the light of the great truths we have been contemplating, I will ask are we acting faithfully,—*how* are we acting towards the destitute and the criminal classes? Are we so much as giving them a cup of cold

---

[1] *L'Assommoir*, par Emile Zola.

water? are we ignoring their condition and putting it out of sight? are we pretending to sigh for wretchedness, while we shun the wretched? Are we, as we devote our sordid lives to making money, of which we shall perhaps dole or fling to them say a thousandth fraction, — are we asking, "Am I my brother's keeper?" If charitable or kind at all, are we more than content with being charitable by substitute and kind *by proxy*? Are we trying to salve our consciences by promiscuous alms, though we know, or might know, that such alms are incredibly pernicious? When we hear the ravages caused by the madness of intemperance, are we contented to sacrifice the well-being of millions to the vested interests of millionaires? Are we only thrusting to the perishing working classes the sponge full of the vinegar of our sham sympathy; and smiling supercilious superiority at the fanatics who are willing to practise some small self-denial while the world standeth, if by doing so they can less make their brothers to offend? We call ourselves Christians. The day was when

Christians *did* something; when their love and their freedom were twin spirits which spread over suffering humanity their healing wings. The early Church, the Mediæval Church, did more than we. In days when rank was well-nigh deified, she made Popes of peasants' sons, and bade Kings hold the stirrups of their mules. In days when the weak were prostrate at the feet of the strong she not only pleaded with the strong for the weak, but made the cause of the weak her own. In days when force was terribly predominant, it was the Church alone which dared to dash down the mailed arm of the baron when it was uplifted to strike his serf. Our problems are less difficult, our work less dangerous; but we do not face them. We leave standing the most horrible streets; we suffer temptation to be sown broadcast with scarce so much as an attempt to check it; we are more afraid of wealth, and capital, and class-interests than our fathers were of the swords of pitiless barbarians, and the wrath of autocratic kings. Surely when we look at the vast problems which face us,—the neglect of which is certain at last to wreak its Nemesis upon us,—when we look at the discontent of the working classes, at the condition of the poor,— we shall see more clearly the duty of not leaving those problems hopelessly unsolved, if we remember that these poorer classes, no less than we, are the sheep of Christ's pasture, and the people of His hand.

ii. Many folds; one flock; one shepherd. Look at the Church. We belong to one fold of it; but when Christ says, "Other sheep I have which are not of this fold," does He not warn us that we are not His only fold; that His flock is wide as humanity; that it is scattered in many folds? How many men try to make an exclusive fold of their own Church! How often have Romanists written as though they excluded all Protestants, and Protestants as though they excluded all Romanists and Churchmen as though they excluded all Dissenters, and Dissenters all Churchmen, almost from the pale of salvation! How has the living

Rock of the blessed Scriptures been broken up into heaps of ruinous missiles! How has the battlefield of theology rung with angry and impotent anathemas! Alas! that men can no longer say, "See how these Christians love one another!" Alas! that the warning should be as needful after nineteen centuries of Christianity, as it was to the Galatian Church, "But if ye bite and devour one another, take heed that ye be not consumed one of another." Whence spring these mutual exasperations, these party collisions, these factious invectives, these "vain word-battlings"? They spring for the most part from the egotism of ignorance; from the pride of system; from the dogmatism of the illiterate; from the intolerance of unchastened hearts and narrow minds. Oh, can we never learn that truth has many aspects; that none of us has any monopoly of it; that very many of those who differ from us may be more sincere, more learned, more holy, more competent than ourselves? Well, at any rate the warning stands, which shows us that we can as easily make an inclosure in God's common air as in His infinite grace—"Other sheep I have which are not of this fold; them also I must bring, and they shall hear my voice."

iii. Many folds; one flock; one shepherd. If it be so with classes, and with Churches, is it not also so with *nations?* In the days of our fathers, it was the fashion of Englishmen and Frenchmen to regard themselves as "natural enemies;" and, partly because of the selfish ambition of Napoleon, Christian nations, armed to the very teeth, watched each other, year after year, with furious detestation. Is there no danger of the same evil spirit arising between England and other nations now? I speak of course in no sense as a politician; I speak only as a Christian, when I deplore this recrudescence of national hatreds. "Sirs, ye are brethren," was the voice of the Church of old to warring kings. It was a voice which utterly condemned the old contemptuous exclusiveness of ancient Greece; the cunning, cruel, tortuous policy of ancient Rome. What, during these long centuries, has been the history of England and Russia? From the Oxus valley, the cradle of the great Aryan race, rolled westward the mighty streams of emigration, that subdued, civilised, and ennobled Europe;—first, the Celtic race; then the Teutonic to which we belong; lastly, the Slavonic or Russian. We, still advancing ever westward, in the fulfilment of our destiny on the track of commerce, traversed half the globe, and reached and conquered India by sea. The Russians, rolling back eastward, as it were, on the old channels of our race, have well-nigh reached the confines of India by land. Ten years ago, speaking in public of events as probable which since have happened, I asked, as I now ask again, "Shall these two Aryan races—the Slav and the Teuton—meet as brothers or as enemies? Shall our intercourse be the intercourse of mutual amity, or of deadly warfare? Let the knowledge of our past history decide us in favour of pacific and beneficent counsels. And so, contemplating the great tidal wave of Aryan migration as it flows and ebbs around our globe, let us see that it be for the blessing of mankind."[1] So I spoke before the Royal Institution ten years ago; and may we not at least aim at this now? Far off I know is the day when war shall be no more; but when I think not only of the horrors of actual war; but of the disturbance of the world's progress by mutual jealousies; and the hindrance to the world's peaceful industries by war's uncertainties; and of the loss to the world's suffering peoples by bloated armaments, then it seems to me that

> "Were half the power which fills the world with terror,
> Were half the wealth bestowed on warring courts,
> Given to redeem the soul from sin and error,
> There were no need of arsenals and forts."

One of the grandest, one of the most Christian of our acts as a great people, in the eyes of generations yet unborn, will be, I think, that in which we, "an old and haughty nation proud in

[1] This is a brief extract from a longer passage devoted to this subject in the second of four lectures delivered before the Royal Institution in March, 1869, and published under the title of "Families of Speech." (Messrs. Longman & Co.)

arms" made of the Bible in very truth our "Statesman's Manual," and applying the lessons of the Sermon on the Mount to the intercourse not of individuals but of continents, by accepting the hostile award of an arbitration, recovered the lost affection, revived the offended brotherhood, of a kindred but alienated power. When we have well learnt the lesson thus to seek peace, then soon shall—

> "The war-drums throb no longer, and the battle flags be furled
> In the parliament of Man, the federation of the world;"

for then indeed shall all Christian nations present the spectacle—dear to heaven if not to earth,—dear to God's purpose if not to man's passion—of one flock, under one shepherd,—and that Shepherd the Prince of Peace.

iv. *Christian* nations?—And are we then to exclude the savage, the barbarian? No! many folds; one flock; one shepherd. The *Scythians* were regarded as the lowest of all barbarians in the days of St. Paul; yet he wrote that, in Christ Jesus, there was neither Jew nor Greek, barbarian, Scythian, bond or free,—but Christ all and in all. Our newspapers talk of our enemies as "morose savages" and "miserable barbarians." Such terms may be correct;—but would not St. Paul have said, in these days, that "in Christ Jesus, there is neither Englishman nor Russian, neither Zulu nor Afghan, but Christ all and in all"? Surely the Huns and Vandals and Visigoths of the early centuries were savage enough; but when the frontiers of the tottering Empire echoed their threatening footsteps, it is Gibbon himself who bears witness that the Church of Christ,—as it had prevailed over the atheism and luxury of ancient civilisation—tamed also the hard hearts of the barbarous invaders. So far from declaring menacingly and contemptuously against them, she won them by her brotherhood, she overawed them with her sanctity. When arms and armies were being swept away before their course, her Bishops checked that course by raising before them the barriers of a moral idea, of a spiritual power; and savages who had seen such types of noble excellence as a Leo and a Benedict,—an Ulphilas and a Severinus,—a Boniface and an Olaf,—were won over by veneration, and by gratitude, to mould themselves, with all that was valuable in the conquered civilisation, into one splendid, permanent, and progressive society. Has modern England, has England in the last two centuries, dealt as faithfully and as Christianly with dusky and savage tribes? Will the Tasmanians, will the Australians, will the Negroes, will the Pacific Islanders, will the North American Indians, will the Maories, will the Hindoos, will the Chinese, have no protests to record, no witness to bear against us on the page of history?

Ah, my brethren, the answer to these questions, be it favourable or unfavourable, is written in the Books of God. Do not think that I am touching on these our present wars and rumours of wars;[1] my thoughts are taking a much wider range. I know that there are good men, and kind-hearted men, and men with

---

[1] This sermon was delivered in April, 1879.

a thousandfold better opportunities of judging than ourselves, who hold that there is grim need that our sons and brothers should be fighting against savages; and this at any rate is no place to discuss the question;—but this I say— that when, for instance, we learnt four days ago how these poor ignorant savages advanced in crowds against our entrenchments;—how the Gatling gun poured its dread volleys upon them; —how they could not pierce our impenetrable veil of fire; how, without their once being able to get within twenty or thirty yards of our camp, while *we* were scarcely touched, 2,000 of them lay stretched on the field of death; oh, then surely I am but speaking the language of every Christian—the language of every good man of whatever politics or party—when I say that such wars are at the very best a most miserable necessity. At least no good man can speak lightly of them; no good man can affect a cynical tone about them; no good man can think that there can be any glory to England from these dreadful responsibilities of her Empire. There was an Indian Mutiny twenty years ago, and terribly we avenged it;[1] but I take it that the day will come when England will carve upon yonder statue of the then Viceroy of India, as his most splendid memorial, the once scornful nickname of "Clemency Canning." The day is coming, I take it, when, alike in the policies of earth, and before the judgment-seat of heaven, the names of Selwyn and Coleridge and Patteson in the Pacific; and of Adoniram Judson in Burmah; and of David Livingstone in Africa; and of Henry Martyn, and Heber, and Cotton in India, shall avail us more than many of those bloody battles, where, for every score of ours, a thousand fall of those other sheep of Christ, which are not of this fold, but who must some day hear His voice.

My brethren, we have swept over a wide range, on this last occasion on which for the present I shall address you; nor will my words be in vain if they lead us, as citizens of England, to meditate humbly on our vast duties

---

[1] Havelock in the Indian Mutiny had to remind his soldiers that "it became not Christians to take heathen butchers for their models." See Marshman's *Life of Havelock*.

as citizens of the City of God. And while, as you will see, I am standing entirely aloof from all political inferences, I beg you not to think these truths unpractical. They are deeply religious if they break the sordid dream of our individual selfishness, and I never speak from this place without feeling how much we might do if but God's fire would touch our hearts. Much—for we are many. You have doubtless seen the beautiful scientific experiment which is called "the superposition of small motions." A large and heavy bar of iron hangs motionless in the air: near it is hung a tiny ball of cork. The little cork is thrown against the iron, for some time with no effect; but each blow of the little ball has awoke a continuous vibration in the iron; and soon it begins to tremble; and then to move; and then to sway; and then to swing strongly to and fro, under the accumulated vibrations of those small but many impacts. So one individual can do but little in a vast society, but the just influence of many individuals, all touching, and all touching again and again, in one direction, is felt irresistibly throughout the mass. If each of us recognised, in our hearts, and in our lives, the brotherhood of man;—the fact that man forms but one flock in different folds under one Shepherd, it would not be long before London would be better; and if London then England; and if England then the world. Is it not an aim worth living for? is it not a task worth effort to hasten the day, when we too, God helping us, may be suffered to take a place, however humble, in that great multitude which no man can number, of all nations, and kindreds, and people, and tongues, standing before the throne, and before the Lamb, in white robes, and palms in their hands;—hungering no more, and thirsting no more, but led to living fountains of waters, ten thousand times ten thousand, and thousands of thousands;—singing praise to Him who has redeemed them by His blood to God?

WORKS BY THE SAME AUTHOR.

NEW AND COLLECTED EDITION OF THE SERMONS, &c.

Crown 8vo. 3s. 6d. each.

Monthly Volumes from December, 1891:—

SEEKERS AFTER GOD. The lives of SENECA, EPICTETUS, and MARCUS AURELIUS. With Illustrations.

ETERNAL HOPE. Sermons in Westminster ABBEY. November and December, 1877.

THE FALL OF MAN : and other Sermons.

THE WITNESS OF HISTORY TO CHRIST. Hulsean Lectures for 1870.

THE SILENCE AND VOICES OF GOD. University and other Sermons.

"IN THE DAYS OF THY YOUTH." Sermons on Practical Subjects, Preached at Marlborough College, from 1871 to 1876.

SAINTLY WORKERS. Lent Lectures delivered at St. Andrew's, Holborn. March and April, 1878.

EPHPHATHA : or, The Amelioration of the WORLD. Sermons preached at Westminster Abbey, with Two Sermons preached in St. Margaret's Church at the Opening of Parliament.

MERCY AND JUDGMENT. A Few Last Words on Christian Eschatology with reference to Dr. Pusey's "What is of Faith?"

SERMONS AND ADDRESSES DELIVERED IN AMERICA. With an Introduction by Bishop PHILLIPS BROOKS.

THE HISTORY OF INTERPRETATION. Being the Bampton Lectures, 1885. Demy 8vo. 16s.

THE MESSAGES OF THE BOOKS. Being Discourses and Notes on the Books of the New Testament. 8vo. 14s.

MACMILLAN & CO., LONDON.

BY THE SAME AUTHOR.

GREEK GRAMMAR RULES, drawn up for the
use of Harrow School. Eighteenth Edition. 8vo. 1s. 6d.

⁎ Now in use in Harrow School, Marlborough College, Rossall School, Uppingham School, Charterhouse School, &c.

A BRIEF GREEK SYNTAX AND HINTS
ON GREEK ACCIDENCE; with some reference to Comparative Philology, and with Illustrations from various Modern Languages. Tenth Edition, 12mo. 4s. 6d.

"Mr. Farrar's volume surpasses all the Greek Grammars we have seen."—*Educational Times.*

"This book is the produce of the ripest scholarship. Though his main object is to treat of Syntax, the space he devotes to comparative philology, and the copious illustrations he gives from various modern languages, increase greatly the value of the book. At the same time his practical experience in teaching his class at Harrow has given him a familiarity with the difficulties that beset beginners, and enable him most successfully to adapt his teaching to their wants. We can most cordially recommend the book."—*Papers for the Schoolmaster.*

LANGUAGE AND LANGUAGES; being
"Chapters on Language" and "Families of Speech." With 2 Philological Maps and 3 Tables of Languages. New Edition. Crown 8vo. 6s.

CHAPTERS ON LANGUAGE.

"Dr. Farrar's volume contains the fruit of much learned thought, and of much study of other learned men's studies. The book is written plainly and intelligibly, and is full of a large human interest."—*Examiner.*

FAMILIES OF SPEECH.

"We fully believe that Dr. Farrar's book is by far the best account as yet given in English, within the same compass, of the history, results, methods, and aspirations of comparative philology or glossology."—*Pall Mall Gazette.*

London : LONGMANS, GREEN, & CO.

THE EARLY DAYS OF CHRISTIANITY.
Ninth Thousand. Two Vols. 24s. Popular Edition, 6s.

THE LIFE AND WORK OF ST. PAUL.
Nineteenth Thousand. Two Vols. 8vo. 24s. Illustrated Edition, 21s. Popular Edition, 6s.

THE LIFE OF CHRIST. Thirty-first
Edition. Library Edition. Two Vols. 8vo. Price 24s. Illustrated Edition, cloth, 21s.; calf or morocco, £2 2s. Popular Edition, 6s. Bijou Edition, 10s. 6d.

MY OBJECT IN LIFE. (Heart Chords
Series.) 1s.

London : CASSELL & COMPANY, LIMITED.

THE GOSPEL OF ST. LUKE. Fcap 8vo.
4s. 6d. (Cambridge Bible for Schools.)

London ; THE CAMBRIDGE WAREHOUSE.

March 1892

A Catalogue

of

Theological Works

published by

Macmillan & Co.

Bedford Street, Strand, London

CONTENTS

THE BIBLE—
    History of the Bible . . . . . .
    Biblical History . . . .
    The Old Testament . . . . . .
    The New Testament . . . . . .

HISTORY OF THE CHRISTIAN CHURCH . . .

THE CHURCH OF ENGLAND . . . . .

DEVOTIONAL BOOKS . . . .

THE FATHERS . . . .

HYMNOLOGY . . . .

SERMONS, LECTURES, ADDRESSES, AND THEOLOGICAL
    ESSAYS . . . .

March 1892.

MACMILLAN AND CO.'S THEOLOGICAL CATALOGUE

The Bible

HISTORY OF THE BIBLE

THE ENGLISH BIBLE: An External and Critical History of the various English Translations of Scripture. By Prof. JOHN EADIE. 2 vols. 8vo. 28s.

THE BIBLE IN THE CHURCH. By Right Rev. Bishop WESTCOTT. 10th Edition. 18mo. 4s. 6d.

BIBLICAL HISTORY

BIBLE LESSONS. By Rev. E. A. ABBOTT. Crown 8vo. 4s. 6d.

SIDE-LIGHTS ON BIBLE HISTORY. By Mrs. SYDNEY BUXTON. Illustrated. Crown 8vo. [*In the Press.*

STORIES FROM THE BIBLE. By Rev. A. J. CHURCH. Illustrated. Two Series. Crown 8vo. 3s. 6d. each.

BIBLE READINGS SELECTED FROM THE PENTATEUCH AND THE BOOK OF JOSHUA. By Rev. J. A. CROSS. 2nd Edition. Globe 8vo. 2s. 6d.

CHILDREN'S TREASURY OF BIBLE STORIES. By Mrs. H. GASKOIN. 18mo. 1s. each. Part I. Old Testament; II. New Testament; III. Three Apostles.

A CLASS-BOOK OF OLD TESTAMENT HISTORY. By Rev. Canon MACLEAR. With Four Maps. 18mo. 4s. 6d.

A CLASS-BOOK OF NEW TESTAMENT HISTORY. Including the connection of the Old and New Testament. By the same. 18mo. 5s. 6d.

A SHILLING BOOK OF OLD TESTAMENT HISTORY. By the same. 18mo. 1s.

A SHILLING BOOK OF NEW TESTAMENT HISTORY. By the same. 18mo. 1s.

THE OLD TESTAMENT

SCRIPTURE READINGS FOR SCHOOLS AND FAMILIES. By C. M. YONGE. Globe 8vo. 1s. 6d. each; also with comments, 3s. 6d. each.—First Series: GENESIS TO DEUTERONOMY.—Second Series: JOSHUA TO SOLOMON.—Third Series: KINGS AND THE PROPHETS.—Fourth Series: THE GOSPEL TIMES.—Fifth Series: APOSTOLIC TIMES.

The Old Testament—*continued.*

THE PATRIARCHS AND LAWGIVERS OF THE OLD TESTAMENT. By FREDERICK DENISON MAURICE. 7th Edition. Crown 8vo. 4s. 6d.

THE PROPHETS AND KINGS OF THE OLD TESTAMENT. By the same. 5th Edition. Crown 8vo. 6s.

THE CANON OF THE OLD TESTAMENT. An Essay on the Growth and Formation of the Hebrew Canon of Scripture. By Rev. Prof. H. E. RYLE. Crown 8vo. [*In the Press.*

The Pentateuch—

AN HISTORICO-CRITICAL INQUIRY INTO THE ORIGIN AND COMPOSITION OF THE HEXATEUCH (PENTATEUCH AND BOOK OF JOSHUA). By Prof. A. KUENEN. Translated by PHILIP H. WICKSTEED, M.A. 8vo. 14s.

The Psalms—

THE PSALMS CHRONOLOGICALLY ARRANGED. An Amended Version, with Historical Introductions and Explanatory Notes. By Four Friends. New Edition. Crown 8vo. 5s. net.

GOLDEN TREASURY PSALTER. The Student's Edition. Being an Edition with briefer Notes of "The Psalms Chronologically Arranged by Four Friends." 18mo. 3s. 6d.

THE PSALMS. With Introductions and Critical Notes. By A. C. JENNINGS, M.A., and W. H. LOWE, M.A. In 2 vols. 2nd Edition. Crown 8vo. 10s. 6d. each.

INTRODUCTION TO THE STUDY AND USE OF THE PSALMS. By Rev. J. F. THRUPP. 2nd Edition. 2 vols. 8vo. 21s.

Isaiah—

ISAIAH XL.—LXVI. With the Shorter Prophecies allied to it. By MATTHEW ARNOLD. With Notes. Crown 8vo. 5s.

ISAIAH OF JERUSALEM. In the Authorised English Version, with Introduction, Corrections, and Notes. By the same. Cr. 8vo. 4s. 6d.

A BIBLE-READING FOR SCHOOLS. The Great Prophecy of Israel's Restoration (Isaiah xl.-lxvi.) Arranged and Edited for Young Learners. By the same. 4th Edition. 18mo. 1s.

COMMENTARY ON THE BOOK OF ISAIAH, Critical, Historical, and Prophetical; including a Revised English Translation. By T. R. BIRKS. 2nd Edition. 8vo. 12s. 6d.

THE BOOK OF ISAIAH CHRONOLOGICALLY ARRANGED. By T. K. CHEYNE. Crown 8vo. 7s. 6d.

Zechariah—

THE HEBREW STUDENT'S COMMENTARY ON ZECHARIAH, Hebrew and LXX. By W. H. LOWE, M.A. 8vo. 10s. 6d.

THE NEW TESTAMENT

THE NEW TESTAMENT. Essay on the Right Estimation of MS. Evidence in the Text of the New Testament. By T. R. BIRKS. Crown 8vo. 3s. 6d.

THE MESSAGES OF THE BOOKS. Being Discourses and Notes on the Books of the New Testament. By Ven. Archdeacon FARRAR. 8vo. 14s.

THE CLASSICAL ELEMENT IN THE NEW TESTAMENT. Considered as a Proof of its Genuineness, with an Appendix on the Oldest Authorities used in the Formation of the Canon. By C. H. HOOLE. 8vo. 10s. 6d.

ON A FRESH REVISION OF THE ENGLISH NEW TESTAMENT. With an Appendix on the last Petition of the Lord's Prayer. By Bishop LIGHTFOOT. Crown 8vo. 7s. 6d.

THE UNITY OF THE NEW TESTAMENT. By F. D. MAURICE. 2nd Edition. 2 vols. Crown 8vo. 12s.

A COMPANION TO THE GREEK TESTAMENT AND THE ENGLISH VERSION. By PHILIP SCHAFF, D.D. Cr. 8vo. 12s.

A GENERAL SURVEY OF THE HISTORY OF THE CANON OF THE NEW TESTAMENT DURING THE FIRST FOUR CENTURIES. By Right Rev. Bishop WESTCOTT. 6th Edition. Crown 8vo. 10s. 6d.

THE NEW TESTAMENT IN THE ORIGINAL GREEK. The Text revised by Bishop WESTCOTT, D.D., and Prof. F. J. A. HORT, D.D. 2 vols. Crown 8vo. 10s. 6d. each.—Vol. I. Text; II. Introduction and Appendix.

THE NEW TESTAMENT IN THE ORIGINAL GREEK, for Schools. The Text revised by Bishop WESTCOTT, D.D., and F. J. A. HORT, D.D. 12mo, cloth, 4s. 6d.; 18mo, roan, red edges, 5s. 6d.; morocco, gilt edges, 6s. 6d.

THE GOSPELS—

THE COMMON TRADITION OF THE SYNOPTIC GOSPELS, in the Text of the Revised Version. By Rev. E. A. ABBOTT and W. G. RUSHBROOKE. Crown 8vo. 3s. 6d.

SYNOPTICON: An Exposition of the Common Matter of the Synoptic Gospels. By W. G. RUSHBROOKE. Printed in Colours. In Six Parts, and Appendix. 4to.—Part I, 3s. 6d. Parts II and III, 7s. Parts IV, V, and VI, with Indices, 10s. 6d. Appendices, 10s. 6d. Complete in 1 vol., 35s. Indispensable to a Theological Student.

INTRODUCTION TO THE STUDY OF THE FOUR GOSPELS. By Right Rev. Bishop WESTCOTT. 7th Ed. Cr. 8vo. 10s. 6d.

THE COMPOSITION OF THE FOUR GOSPELS. By Rev. ARTHUR WRIGHT. Crown 8vo. 5s.

Gospel of St. Matthew—

THE GOSPEL ACCORDING TO ST. MATTHEW. Greek Text as Revised by Bishop WESTCOTT and Dr. HORT. With Introduction and Notes by Rev. A. SLOMAN, M.A. Fcap. 8vo. 2s. 6d.

CHOICE NOTES ON ST. MATTHEW, drawn from Old and New Sources. Crown 8vo. 4s. 6d. (St. Matthew and St. Mark in 1 vol. 9s.)

Gospel of St. Mark—
SCHOOL READINGS IN THE GREEK TESTAMENT. Being the Outlines of the Life of our Lord as given by St. Mark, with additions from the Text of the other Evangelists. Edited, with Notes and Vocabulary, by Rev. A. CALVERT, M.A. Fcap. 8vo. 2s. 6d.
CHOICE NOTES ON ST. MARK, drawn from Old and New Sources. Cr. 8vo. 4s. 6d. (St. Matthew and St. Mark in 1 vol. 9s.)

Gospel of St. Luke—
THE GOSPEL ACCORDING TO ST. LUKE. The Greek Text as Revised by Bishop WESTCOTT and Dr. HORT. With Introduction and Notes by Rev. J. BOND, M.A. Fcap. 8vo. 2s. 6d.
CHOICE NOTES ON ST. LUKE, drawn from Old and New Sources. Crown 8vo. 4s. 6d.
THE GOSPEL OF THE KINGDOM OF HEAVEN. A Course of Lectures on the Gospel of St. Luke. By F. D. MAURICE. 3rd Edition. Crown 8vo. 6s.

Gospel of St. John—
THE GOSPEL OF ST. JOHN. By F. D. MAURICE. 8th Ed. Cr. 8vo. 6s.
CHOICE NOTES ON ST. JOHN, drawn from Old and New Sources. Crown 8vo. 4s. 6d.

THE ACTS OF THE APOSTLES—
THE ACTS OF THE APOSTLES. Being the Greek Text as Revised by Bishop WESTCOTT and Dr. HORT. With Explanatory Notes by T. E. PAGE, M.A. Fcap. 8vo. 3s. 6d.
THE CHURCH OF THE FIRST DAYS. THE CHURCH OF JERUSALEM. THE CHURCH OF THE GENTILES. THE CHURCH OF THE WORLD. Lectures on the Acts of the Apostles. By Very Rev. C. J. VAUGHAN. Crown 8vo. 10s. 6d.

THE EPISTLES of St. Paul—
ST. PAUL'S EPISTLE TO THE ROMANS. The Greek Text, with English Notes. By Very Rev. C. J. VAUGHAN. 7th Edition. Crown 8vo. 7s. 6d.
A COMMENTARY ON ST. PAUL'S TWO EPISTLES TO THE CORINTHIANS. Greek Text, with Commentary. By Rev. W. KAY. 8vo. 9s.
ST. PAUL'S EPISTLE TO THE GALATIANS. A Revised Text, with Introduction, Notes, and Dissertations. By Bishop LIGHTFOOT. 10th Edition. 8vo. 12s.
ST. PAUL'S EPISTLE TO THE PHILIPPIANS. A Revised Text, with Introduction, Notes, and Dissertations. By the same. 9th Edition. 8vo. 12s.
ST. PAUL'S EPISTLE TO THE PHILIPPIANS. With translation, Paraphrase, and Notes for English Readers. By Very Rev. C. J. VAUGHAN. Crown 8vo. 5s.
ST. PAUL'S EPISTLES TO THE COLOSSIANS AND TO PHILEMON. A Revised Text, with Introductions, etc. By Bishop LIGHTFOOT. 9th Edition. 8vo. 12s.

Of St. Paul—*continued.*
    THE EPISTLES OF ST. PAUL TO THE EPHESIANS, THE COLOSSIANS, AND PHILEMON. With Introductions and Notes. By Rev. J. LL. DAVIES. 2nd Edition. 8vo. 7s. 6d.
    THE EPISTLES OF ST. PAUL. For English Readers. Part I, containing the First Epistle to the Thessalonians. By Very Rev. C. J. VAUGHAN. 2nd Edition. 8vo. Sewed. 1s. 6d.
    ST. PAUL'S EPISTLES TO THE THESSALONIANS, COMMENTARY ON THE GREEK TEXT. By Prof. JOHN EADIE. 8vo. 12s.

The Epistle of St. James—
    ST. JAMES' EPISTLE. The Greek Text, with Introduction and Notes. By Rev. JOSEPH MAYOR, M.A. 8vo. [*In the Press.*

The Epistles of St. John—
    THE EPISTLES OF ST. JOHN. By F. D. MAURICE. 4th Edition. Crown 8vo. 6s.
    THE EPISTLES OF ST. JOHN. The Greek Text, with Notes. By Right Rev. Bishop WESTCOTT. 2nd Edition. 8vo. 12s. 6d.

The Epistle to the Hebrews—
    THE EPISTLE TO THE HEBREWS IN GREEK AND ENGLISH. With Notes. By Rev. FREDERIC RENDALL. Crown 8vo. 6s.
    THE EPISTLE TO THE HEBREWS. English Text, with Commentary. By the same. Crown 8vo. 7s. 6d.
    THE EPISTLE TO THE HEBREWS. With Notes. By Very Rev. C. J. VAUGHAN. Crown 8vo. 7s. 6d.
    THE EPISTLE TO THE HEBREWS. The Greek Text, with Notes and Essays. By Right Rev. Bishop WESTCOTT. 8vo. 14s.

REVELATION—
    LECTURES ON THE APOCALYPSE. By F. D. MAURICE. 2nd Edition. Crown 8vo. 6s.
    THE REVELATION OF ST. JOHN. By Rev. Prof. W. MILLIGAN. 2nd Edition. Crown 8vo. 7s. 6d.
    LECTURES ON THE REVELATION OF ST. JOHN. By Very Rev. C. J. VAUGHAN. 5th Edition. Crown 8vo. 10s. 6d.

THE BIBLE WORD-BOOK. By W. ALDIS WRIGHT. 2nd Edition. Crown 8vo. 7s. 6d.

Christian Church, History of the

Church (Dean).—THE OXFORD MOVEMENT. Twelve Years, 1833-45. Globe 8vo. 5s.
Cunningham (Rev. John).—THE GROWTH OF THE CHURCH IN ITS ORGANISATION AND INSTITUTIONS. 8vo. 9s.
Dale (A. W. W.)—THE SYNOD OF ELVIRA, AND CHRISTIAN LIFE IN THE FOURTH CENTURY. Cr. 8vo. 10s. 6d.

Hardwick (Archdeacon).—A HISTORY OF THE CHRISTIAN CHURCH. Middle Age. Ed. by Bishop STUBBS. Cr. 8vo. 10s. 6d.
A HISTORY OF THE CHRISTIAN CHURCH DURING THE REFORMATION. Revised by Bishop STUBBS. Cr. 8vo. 10s. 6d.

Hort (Dr. F. J. A.)—TWO DISSERTATIONS. I. On ΜΟΝΟΓΕΝΗΣ ΘΕΟΣ in Scripture and Tradition. II. On the "Constantinopolitan" Creed and other Eastern Creeds of the Fourth Century. 8vo. 7s. 6d.

Killen (W. D.)—ECCLESIASTICAL HISTORY OF IRELAND, FROM THE EARLIEST DATE TO THE PRESENT TIME. 2 vols. 8vo. 25s.

Simpson (W.)—AN EPITOME OF THE HISTORY OF THE CHRISTIAN CHURCH. Fcap. 8vo. 3s. 6d.

Vaughan (Very Rev. C. J., Dean of Llandaff).—THE CHURCH OF THE FIRST DAYS. THE CHURCH OF JERUSALEM. THE CHURCH OF THE GENTILES. THE CHURCH OF THE WORLD. Crown 8vo. 10s. 6d.

Ward (W.)—WILLIAM GEORGE WARD AND THE OXFORD MOVEMENT. Portrait. 8vo. 14s.

The Church of England

Catechism of—
A CLASS-BOOK OF THE CATECHISM OF THE CHURCH OF ENGLAND. By Rev. Canon MACLEAR. 18mo. 1s. 6d.
A FIRST CLASS-BOOK OF THE CATECHISM OF THE CHURCH OF ENGLAND, with Scripture Proofs for Junior Classes and Schools. By the same. 18mo. 6d.
THE ORDER OF CONFIRMATION, with Prayers and Devotions. By the Rev. Canon MACLEAR. 32mo. 6d.

Collects—
COLLECTS OF THE CHURCH OF ENGLAND. With a Coloured Floral Design to each Collect. Crown 8vo. 12s.

Disestablishment—
DISESTABLISHMENT AND DISENDOWMENT. What are they? By Prof. E. A. FREEMAN. 4th Edition. Crown 8vo. 1s.
DISESTABLISHMENT: or, A Defence of the Principle of a National Church. By GEORGE HARWOOD. 8vo. 12s.
A DEFENCE OF THE CHURCH OF ENGLAND AGAINST DISESTABLISHMENT. By ROUNDELL, EARL OF SELBORNE. Crown 8vo. 2s. 6d.
ANCIENT FACTS & FICTIONS CONCERNING CHURCHES AND TITHES. By the same. 2nd Edition. Crown 8vo. 7s. 6d.

Dissent in its Relation to—
DISSENT IN ITS RELATION TO THE CHURCH OF ENGLAND. By Rev. G. H. CURTEIS. Bampton Lectures for 1871. Crown 8vo. 7s. 6d.

Holy Communion—
　THE COMMUNION SERVICE FROM THE BOOK OF COMMON PRAYER, with Select Readings from the Writings of the Rev. F. D. MAURICE. Edited by Bishop COLENSO. 6th Edition. 16mo. 2s. 6d.
　BEFORE THE TABLE: An Inquiry, Historical and Theological, into the Meaning of the Consecration Rubric in the Communion Service of the Church of England. By Very Rev. J. S. HOWSON. 8vo. 7s. 6d.
　FIRST COMMUNION, with Prayers and Devotions for the newly Confirmed. By Rev. Canon MACLEAR. 32mo. 6d.
　A MANUAL OF INSTRUCTION FOR CONFIRMATION AND FIRST COMMUNION, with Prayers and Devotions. By the same. 32mo. 2s.

Liturgy—
　A COMPANION TO THE LECTIONARY. By Rev. W. BENHAM, B.D. Crown 8vo. 4s. 6d.
　AN INTRODUCTION TO THE CREEDS. By Rev. Canon MACLEAR. 18mo. 3s. 6d.
　AN INTRODUCTION TO THE THIRTY-NINE ARTICLES. By the same. 18mo. [*In the Press.*
　A HISTORY OF THE BOOK OF COMMON PRAYER. By Rev. F. PROCTER. 18th Edition. Crown 8vo. 10s. 6d.
　AN ELEMENTARY INTRODUCTION TO THE BOOK OF COMMON PRAYER. By Rev. F. PROCTER and Rev. Canon MACLEAR. 18mo. 2s. 6d.
　TWELVE DISCOURSES ON SUBJECTS CONNECTED WITH THE LITURGY AND WORSHIP OF THE CHURCH OF ENGLAND. By Very Rev. C. J. VAUGHAN. 4th Edition. Fcap. 8vo. 6s.

Devotional Books

Brooke (S. A.)—FORM OF MORNING AND EVENING PRAYER, and for the Administration of the Lord's Supper, together with the Baptismal and Marriage Services, Bedford Chapel, Bloomsbury. Fcap. 8vo. 1s. net.

Eastlake (Lady).—FELLOWSHIP: LETTERS ADDRESSED TO MY SISTER-MOURNERS. Crown 8vo. 2s. 6d.

IMITATIO CHRISTI, LIBRI IV. Printed in Borders after Holbein, Dürer, and other old Masters, containing Dances of Death, Acts of Mercy, Emblems, etc. Crown 8vo. 7s. 6d.

Kingsley (Charles).—OUT OF THE DEEP: WORDS FOR THE SORROWFUL. From the writings of CHARLES KINGSLEY. Extra fcap. 8vo. 3s. 6d.
　DAILY THOUGHTS. Selected from the Writings of CHARLES KINGSLEY. By his Wife. Crown 8vo. 6s.

FROM DEATH TO LIFE. Fragments of Teaching to a Village Congregation. With Letters on the "Life after Death." Edited by his Wife. Fcap. 8vo. 2s. 6d.

Maclear (Rev. Canon).—A MANUAL OF INSTRUCTION FOR CONFIRMATION AND FIRST COMMUNION, WITH PRAYERS AND DEVOTIONS. 32mo. 2s.

THE HOUR OF SORROW; OR, THE OFFICE FOR THE BURIAL OF THE DEAD. 32mo. 2s.

Maurice (Frederick Denison).—LESSONS OF HOPE. Readings from the Works of F. D. MAURICE. Selected by Rev. J. LL. DAVIES, M.A. Crown 8vo. 5s.

RAYS OF SUNLIGHT FOR DARK DAYS. With a Preface by Very Rev. C. J. VAUGHAN, D.D. New Edition. 18mo. 3s. 6d.

Service (Rev. John).—PRAYERS FOR PUBLIC WORSHIP. Crown 8vo. 4s. 6d.

THE WORSHIP OF GOD, AND FELLOWSHIP AMONG MEN. By FREDERICK DENISON MAURICE and others. Fcap. 8vo. 3s. 6d.

Welby-Gregory (The Hon. Lady).—LINKS AND CLUES. 2nd Edition. Crown 8vo. 6s.

Westcott (Rt. Rev. B. F., Bishop of Durham).—THOUGHTS ON REVELATION AND LIFE. Selections from the Writings of Bishop WESTCOTT. Edited by Rev. S. PHILLIPS. Crown 8vo. 6s.

Wilbraham (Frances M.)—IN THE SERE AND YELLOW LEAF: THOUGHTS AND RECOLLECTIONS FOR OLD AND YOUNG. Globe 8vo. 3s. 6d.

The Fathers

Cunningham (Rev. W.)—THE EPISTLE OF ST. BARNABAS. A Dissertation, including a Discussion of its Date and Authorship. Together with the Greek Text, the Latin Version, and a New English Translation and Commentary. Crown 8vo. 7s. 6d.

Donaldson (Prof. James).—THE APOSTOLICAL FATHERS. A Critical Account of their Genuine Writings, and of their Doctrines. 2nd Edition. Crown 8vo. 7s. 6d.

Lightfoot (Bishop).—THE APOSTOLIC FATHERS. Part I. ST. CLEMENT OF ROME. Revised Texts, with Introductions, Notes, Dissertations, and Translations. 2 vols. 8vo. 32s.

THE APOSTOLIC FATHERS. Part II. ST. IGNATIUS to ST. POLYCARP. Revised Texts, with Introductions, Notes, Dissertations, and Translations. 3 vols. 2nd Edition. Demy 8vo. 48s.

THE APOSTOLIC FATHERS. Abridged Edition. With Short Introductions, Greek Text, and English Translation. 8vo. 16s.

Hymnology

Brooke (S. A.)—CHRISTIAN HYMNS. Edited and arranged. Fcap. 8vo. 2s. net.
This may also be had bound up with the Form of Service at Bedford Chapel, Bloomsbury. Price complete, 3s. net.

Palgrave (Prof. F. T.)—ORIGINAL HYMNS. 18mo. 1s. 6d.

Selborne (Roundell, Earl of)—
THE BOOK OF PRAISE. From the best English Hymn Writers. 18mo. 2s. 6d. net.
A HYMNAL. Chiefly from *The Book of Praise*. In various sizes.—A. Royal 32mo. 6d.—B. Small 18mo, larger type. 1s.—C. Same Edition, fine paper. 1s. 6d.—An Edition with Music, Selected, Harmonised, and Composed by JOHN HULLAH. Square 18mo. 3s. 6d.

Woods (M. A.)—HYMNS FOR SCHOOL WORSHIP. Compiled by M. A. WOODS. 18mo. 1s. 6d.

Sermons, Lectures, Addresses, and Theological Essays

(See also 'Bible,' 'Church of England,' 'Fathers.')

Abbot (Francis)—
SCIENTIFIC THEISM. Crown 8vo. 7s. 6d.
THE WAY OUT OF AGNOSTICISM : or, The Philosophy of Free Religion. Crown 8vo. 4s. 6d.

Abbott (Rev. E. A.)—
CAMBRIDGE SERMONS. 8vo. 6s.
OXFORD SERMONS. 8vo. 7s. 6d.
PHILOMYTHUS. An Antidote against Credulity. A discussion of Cardinal Newman's Essay on Ecclesiastical Miracles. 2nd Edition. Crown 8vo. 3s. 6d.
NEWMANIANISM. A Reply. Crown 8vo. Sewed, 1s. net.

Ainger (Rev. Alfred, Canon of Bristol).—SERMONS PREACHED IN THE TEMPLE CHURCH. Extra fcap. 8vo. 6s.

Alexander (W., Bishop of Derry and Raphoe).—THE LEADING IDEAS OF THE GOSPELS. New Edition, Revised and Enlarged. Crown 8vo. 6s.

Baines (Rev. Edward).—SERMONS. With a Preface and Memoir, by A. BARRY, D.D., late Bishop of Sydney. Crown 8vo. 6s.

Barry (A.)—FIRST WORDS IN AUSTRALIA : Sermons. Crown 8vo. 5s.

Bather (Archdeacon).—ON SOME MINISTERIAL DUTIES, CATECHISING, PREACHING, ETC. Edited, with a Preface, by Very Rev. C. J. VAUGHAN, D.D. Fcap. 8vo. 4s. 6d.

Bernard (Canon T. D.)—THE CENTRAL TEACHING OF CHRIST. Being a Study and Exposition of St. John, Chapters XIII. to XVII. inclusive. Crown 8vo. [*In the Press.*

Binnie (Rev. William).—SERMONS. Crown 8vo. 6s.

Birks (Thomas Rawson)—
THE DIFFICULTIES OF BELIEF IN CONNECTION WITH THE CREATION AND THE FALL, REDEMPTION, AND JUDGMENT. 2nd Edition. Crown 8vo. 5s.
JUSTIFICATION AND IMPUTED RIGHTEOUSNESS. Being a Review of Ten Sermons on the Nature and Effects of Faith, by JAMES THOMAS O'BRIEN, D.D., late Bishop of Ossory, Ferns, and Leighlin. Crown 8vo. 6s.
SUPERNATURAL REVELATION: or, First Principles of Moral Theology. 8vo. 8s.

Brooke (Rev. Stopford A.)—SHORT SERMONS. Cr. 8vo. 6s.

Brooks (Phillips, Bishop of Massachusetts)—
THE CANDLE OF THE LORD, and other Sermons. Crown 8vo. 6s.
SERMONS PREACHED IN ENGLISH CHURCHES. Crown 8vo. 6s.
TWENTY SERMONS. Crown 8vo. 6s.
TOLERANCE. Crown 8vo. 2s. 6d.
THE LIGHT OF THE WORLD. Crown 8vo. 3s. 6d.

Brunton (T. Lauder). — THE BIBLE AND SCIENCE. With Illustrations. Crown 8vo. 10s. 6d.

Butler (Rev. George).—SERMONS PREACHED IN CHELTENHAM COLLEGE CHAPEL. 8vo. 7s. 6d.

Butler (W. Archer)—
SERMONS, DOCTRINAL AND PRACTICAL. 11th Edition. 8vo. 8s.
SECOND SERIES OF SERMONS. 8vo. 7s.

Calderwood (Rev. Prof.)—
THE RELATIONS OF SCIENCE AND RELIGION. Crown 8vo. 5s.
THE PARABLES OF OUR LORD. Crown 8vo. 6s.

Campbell (Dr. John M'Leod)—
THE NATURE OF THE ATONEMENT. 6th Ed. Cr. 8vo. 6s.
REMINISCENCES AND REFLECTIONS. Edited with an Introductory Narrative, by his Son, DONALD CAMPBELL, M.A. Crown 8vo. 7s. 6d.
THOUGHTS ON REVELATION. 2nd Edition. Crown 8vo. 5s.
RESPONSIBILITY FOR THE GIFT OF ETERNAL LIFE. Compiled from Sermons preached at Row, in the years 1829-31. Crown 8vo. 5s.

Canterbury (Edward White, Archbishop of)—
  BOY-LIFE: its Trial, its Strength, its Fulness. Sundays in Wellington College, 1859-73. 4th Edition. Crown 8vo. 6s.
  THE SEVEN GIFTS. Addressed to the Diocese of Canterbury in his Primary Visitation. 2nd Edition. Crown 8vo. 6s.
  CHRIST AND HIS TIMES. Addressed to the Diocese of Canterbury in his Second Visitation. Crown 8vo. 6s.
  A PASTORAL LETTER TO THE DIOCESE OF CANTERBURY. Written at the request of the Archdeacons and Rural Deans. Dec. 1890. 8vo, sewed. 1d.

Carpenter (W. Boyd, Bishop of Ripon)—
  TRUTH IN TALE. Addresses, chiefly to Children. Crown 8vo. 4s. 6d.
  THE PERMANENT ELEMENTS OF RELIGION: Bampton Lectures, 1887. 2nd Edition. Crown 8vo. 6s.

Cazenove (J. Gibson).—CONCERNING THE BEING AND ATTRIBUTES OF GOD. 8vo. 5s.

Church (Dean)—
  THE OXFORD MOVEMENT. Twelve Years, 1833-45. Globe 8vo. 5s.
  HUMAN LIFE AND ITS CONDITIONS. Crown 8vo. 6s.
  THE GIFTS OF CIVILISATION, and other Sermons and Lectures. 2nd Edition. Crown 8vo. 7s. 6d.
  DISCIPLINE OF THE CHRISTIAN CHARACTER, and other Sermons. Crown 8vo. 4s. 6d.
  ADVENT SERMONS. 1885. Crown 8vo. 4s. 6d.
  VILLAGE SERMONS. Crown 8vo. 6s.
  CLERGYMAN'S SELF-EXAMINATION CONCERNING THE APOSTLES' CREED. Extra fcap. 8vo. 1s. 6d.

Congreve (Rev. John).—HIGH HOPES AND PLEADINGS FOR A REASONABLE FAITH, NOBLER THOUGHTS, LARGER CHARITY. Crown 8vo. 5s.

Cooke (Josiah P., Jun.)—RELIGION AND CHEMISTRY. Crown 8vo. 7s. 6d.

Cotton (Bishop).—SERMONS PREACHED TO ENGLISH CONGREGATIONS IN INDIA. Crown 8vo. 7s. 6d.

Cunningham (Rev. W.)—CHRISTIAN CIVILISATION, WITH SPECIAL REFERENCE TO INDIA. Cr. 8vo. 5s.

Curteis (Rev. G. H.)—THE SCIENTIFIC OBSTACLES TO CHRISTIAN BELIEF. The Boyle Lectures, 1884. Cr. 8vo. 6s.

Davies (Rev. J. Llewelyn)—
  THE GOSPEL AND MODERN LIFE. 2nd Edition, to which is added Morality according to the Sacrament of the Lord's Supper. Extra fcap. 8vo. 6s.
  SOCIAL QUESTIONS FROM THE POINT OF VIEW OF CHRISTIAN THEOLOGY. 2nd Edition. Crown 8vo. 6s.

Davies (Rev. J. Llewelyn)—*continued.*
  WARNINGS AGAINST SUPERSTITION. Extra fcap. 8vo. 2s. 6d.
  THE CHRISTIAN CALLING. Extra fcap. 8vo. 6s.
  ORDER AND GROWTH AS INVOLVED IN THE SPIRITUAL CONSTITUTION OF HUMAN SOCIETY. Crown 8vo. 3s. 6d.
  BAPTISM, CONFIRMATION, AND THE LORD'S SUPPER, as interpreted by their Outward Signs. Three Addresses. New Edition. 18mo. 1s.

Diggle (Rev. J. W.)—GODLINESS AND MANLINESS. A Miscellany of Brief Papers touching the Relation of Religion to Life. Crown 8vo. 6s.

Drummond (Prof. James).—INTRODUCTION TO THE STUDY OF THEOLOGY. Crown 8vo. 5s.
  ECCE HOMO. A Survey of the Life and Work of Jesus Christ. 20th Edition. Globe 8vo. 6s.

Ellerton (Rev. John).—THE HOLIEST MANHOOD, AND ITS LESSONS FOR BUSY LIVES. Crown 8vo. 6s.
  FAITH AND CONDUCT: An Essay on Verifiable Religion. Crown 8vo. 7s. 6d.

Farrar (Ven. F. W., Archdeacon of Westminster)—
  MERCY AND JUDGMENT. A few last words on Christian Eschatology. 2nd Edition. Crown 8vo. 10s. 6d.
  THE SILENCE AND VOICES OF GOD. University and other Sermons. 7th Edition. Crown 8vo. 6s.
  IN THE DAYS OF THY YOUTH. Sermons on Practical Subjects, preached at Marlborough College. 9th Edition. Crown 8vo. 9s.
  EPHPHATHA: or, The !Amelioration of the World. Sermons preached at Westminster Abbey. Crown 8vo. 6s.
  SERMONS AND ADDRESSES delivered in America. Crown 8vo. 7s. 6d.
  THE WITNESS OF HISTORY TO CHRIST. Being the Hulsean Lectures for 1870. 7th Edition. Crown 8vo. 5s.
  SAINTLY WORKERS. Five Lenten Lectures. 3rd Edition. Crown 8vo. 6s.
  THE HISTORY OF INTERPRETATION. Being the Bampton Lectures, 1885. 8vo. 16s.

  New and Collected Edition of the Sermons, etc. Crown 8vo. 3s. 6d. each. Monthly volumes from *December* 1891.
  SEEKERS AFTER GOD.
  ETERNAL HOPE. Sermons Preached in Westminster Abbey.
  THE FALL OF MAN, and other Sermons.
  THE WITNESS OF HISTORY TO CHRIST. Hulsean Lectures.
  THE SILENCE AND VOICES OF GOD.
  IN THE DAYS OF THY YOUTH. Sermons on Practical Subjects.
  SAINTLY WORKERS. Five Lenten Lectures.
  EPHPHATHA: or, The Amelioration of the World.

Farrar (Ven. F. W., Archdeacon of Westminster).—*continued.*
MERCY AND JUDGMENT. A few last words on Christian Eschatology.
SERMONS AND ADDRESSES delivered in America.

Fiske (John).—MAN'S DESTINY VIEWED IN THE LIGHT OF HIS ORIGIN. Crown 8vo. 3s. 6d.

Forbes (Rev. Granville).—THE VOICE OF GOD IN THE PSALMS. Crown 8vo. 6s. 6d.

Fowle (Rev. T. W.)—A NEW ANALOGY BETWEEN REVEALED RELIGION AND THE COURSE AND CONSTITUTION OF NATURE. Crown 8vo. 6s.

Fraser (Bishop).—SERMONS. Edited by Rev. JOHN W. DIGGLE. 2 vols. Crown 8vo. 6s. each.

Hamilton (John)—
ON TRUTH AND ERROR. Crown 8vo. 5s.
ARTHUR'S SEAT: or, The Church of the Banned. Crown 8vo. 6s.
ABOVE AND AROUND: Thoughts on God and Man. 12mo. 2s. 6d.

Hardwick (Archdeacon).—CHRIST AND OTHER MASTERS. 6th Edition. Crown 8vo. 10s. 6d.

Hare (Julius Charles)—
THE MISSION OF THE COMFORTER. New Edition. Edited by Dean PLUMPTRE. Crown 8vo. 7s. 6d.
THE VICTORY OF FAITH. Edited by Dean PLUMPTRE, with Introductory Notices by Prof. MAURICE and Dean STANLEY. Crown 8vo. 6s. 6d.

Harper (Father Thomas, S.J.)—THE METAPHYSICS OF THE SCHOOL. In 5 vols. Vols. I. and II. 8vo. 18s. each. Vol. III. Part I. 12s.

Harris (Rev. G. C.)—SERMONS. With a Memoir by CHARLOTTE M. YONGE, and Portrait. Extra fcap. 8vo. 6s.

Hutton (R. H.)—
ESSAYS ON SOME OF THE MODERN GUIDES OF ENGLISH THOUGHT IN MATTERS OF FAITH. Globe 8vo. 6s.
THEOLOGICAL ESSAYS. Globe 8vo. 6s.

Illingworth (Rev. J. R.)—SERMONS PREACHED IN A COLLEGE CHAPEL. Crown 8vo. 5s.

Jacob (Rev. J. A.)—BUILDING IN SILENCE, and other Sermons. Extra fcap. 8vo. 6s.

James (Rev. Herbert).—THE COUNTRY CLERGYMAN AND HIS WORK. Crown 8vo. 6s.

Jeans (Rev. G. E.)—HAILEYBURY CHAPEL, and other Sermons. Fcap. 8vo. 3s. 6d.

Jellett (Rev. Dr.)—
THE ELDER SON, and other Sermons. Crown 8vo. 6s.
THE EFFICACY OF PRAYER. 3rd Edition. Crown 8vo. 5s.

Kellogg (Rev. S. H.)—THE LIGHT OF ASIA AND THE LIGHT OF THE WORLD. Crown 8vo. 7s. 6d.

Kingsley (Charles)—
VILLAGE AND TOWN AND COUNTRY SERMONS. Crown 8vo. 3s. 6d.
THE WATER OF LIFE, and other Sermons. Crown 8vo. 3s. 6d.
SERMONS ON NATIONAL SUBJECTS, AND THE KING OF THE EARTH. Crown 8vo. 3s. 6d.
SERMONS FOR THE TIMES. Crown 8vo. 3s. 6d.
GOOD NEWS OF GOD. Crown 8vo. 3s. 6d.
THE GOSPEL OF THE PENTATEUCH, AND DAVID. Crown 8vo. 3s. 6d.
DISCIPLINE, and other Sermons. Crown 8vo. 3s. 6d.
WESTMINSTER SERMONS. Crown 8vo. 3s. 6d.
ALL SAINTS' DAY, and other Sermons. Crown 8vo. 3s. 6d.

Kirkpatrick (Prof. A. F.)—THE DIVINE LIBRARY OF THE OLD TESTAMENT. Its Origin, Preservation, Inspiration, and Permanent Value. Crown 8vo. 3s. net.

Kynaston (Rev. Herbert, D.D.)—SERMONS PREACHED IN THE COLLEGE CHAPEL, CHELTENHAM. Crown 8vo. 6s.

Lightfoot (Bishop)—
LEADERS IN THE NORTHERN CHURCH: Sermons Preached in the Diocese of Durham. 2nd Edition. Crown 8vo. 6s.
ORDINATION ADDRESSES AND COUNSELS TO CLERGY. Crown 8vo. 6s.
CAMBRIDGE SERMONS. Crown 8vo. 6s.
SERMONS PREACHED IN ST. PAUL'S CATHEDRAL. Crown 8vo. 6s.
SERMONS PREACHED ON SPECIAL OCCASIONS. Crown 8vo. 6s.
A CHARGE DELIVERED TO THE CLERGY OF THE DIOCESE OF DURHAM, 25th Nov. 1886. Demy 8vo. 2s.
ESSAYS ON THE WORK ENTITLED "Supernatural Religion." 8vo. 10s. 6d.
ESSAYS. In Two Vols. (1) Dissertations on the Apostolic Age. (2) Miscellaneous. 8vo. [*In the Press.*

Maclaren (Rev. Alexander)—
SERMONS PREACHED AT MANCHESTER. 11th Edition. Fcap. 8vo. 4s. 6d.
A SECOND SERIES OF SERMONS. 7th Ed. Fcap. 8vo. 4s. 6d.
A THIRD SERIES. 6th Edition. Fcap. 8vo. 4s. 6d.
WEEK-DAY EVENING ADDRESSES. 4th Ed. Fcap. 8vo. 2s. 6d.
THE SECRET OF POWER, AND OTHER SERMONS. Fcap. 8vo. 4s. 6d.

Macmillan (Rev. Hugh)—
BIBLE TEACHINGS IN NATURE. 15th Ed. Globe 8vo. 6s.
THE TRUE VINE; OR, THE ANALOGIES OF OUR LORD'S ALLEGORY. 5th Edition. Globe 8vo. 6s.
THE MINISTRY OF NATURE. 8th Edition. Globe 8vo. 6s.

Macmillan (Rev. Hugh)—*continued.*
 THE SABBATH OF THE FIELDS. 6th Edition. Globe 8vo. 6s.
 THE MARRIAGE IN CANA. Globe 8vo. 6s.
 TWO WORLDS ARE OURS. 3rd Edition. Globe 8vo. 6s.
 THE OLIVE LEAF. Globe 8vo. 6s.
 THE GATE BEAUTIFUL AND OTHER BIBLE TEACHINGS FOR THE YOUNG. Crown 8vo. 3s. 6d.
Mahaffy (Rev. Prof.)—THE DECAY OF MODERN PREACHING: AN ESSAY. Crown 8vo. 3s. 6d.
Maturin (Rev. W.)—THE BLESSEDNESS OF THE DEAD IN CHRIST. Crown 8vo. 7s. 6d.
Maurice (Frederick Denison)—
 THE KINGDOM OF CHRIST. 3rd. Ed. 2 Vols. Cr. 8vo. 12s.
 EXPOSITORY SERMONS ON THE PRAYER-BOOK; AND ON THE LORD'S PRAYER. New Edition. Crown 8vo. 6s.
 SERMONS PREACHED IN COUNTRY CHURCHES. 2nd Edition. Crown 8vo. 6s.
 THE CONSCIENCE. Lectures on Casuistry. 3rd Ed. Cr. 8vo. 4s. 6d.
 DIALOGUES ON FAMILY WORSHIP. Crown 8vo. 4s. 6d.
 THE DOCTRINE OF SACRIFICE DEDUCED FROM THE SCRIPTURES. 2nd Edition. Crown 8vo. 6s.
 THE RELIGIONS OF THE WORLD. 6th Edition. Cr. 8vo. 4s. 6d.
 ON THE SABBATH DAY; THE CHARACTER OF THE WARRIOR; AND ON THE INTERPRETATION OF HISTORY. Fcap. 8vo. 2s. 6d.
 LEARNING AND WORKING. Crown 8vo. 4s. 6d.
 THE LORD'S PRAYER, THE CREED, AND THE COMMANDMENTS. 18mo. 1s.
 THEOLOGICAL ESSAYS. 4th Edition. Crown 8vo. 6s.
 SERMONS PREACHED IN LINCOLN'S INN CHAPEL. In Six Volumes. Crown 8vo. 3s. 6d. each. Monthly from October 1891.
Milligan (Rev. Prof. W.)—THE RESURRECTION OF OUR LORD. Fourth Thousand. Crown 8vo. 5s.
 THE ASCENSION AND HEAVENLY PRIESTHOOD OF OUR LORD. *Baird Lectures,* 1891. Crown 8vo. 7s. 6d.
 LECTURES ON THE APOCALYPSE. Cr. 8vo. 5s.
Moorhouse (J., Bishop of Manchester)—
 JACOB: Three Sermons. Extra fcap. 8vo. 3s. 6d.
 THE TEACHING OF CHRIST. Its Conditions, Secret, and Results. Crown 8vo. 3s. net.
Mylne (L. G., Bishop of Bombay).—SERMONS PREACHED IN ST. THOMAS'S CATHEDRAL, BOMBAY. Crown 8vo. 6s.
NATURAL RELIGION. By the author of "Ecce Homo." 3rd Edition. Globe 8vo. 6s.
Pattison (Mark).—SERMONS. Crown 8vo. 6s.
PAUL OF TARSUS. 8vo. 10s. 6d.
PHILOCHRISTUS. Memoirs of a Disciple of the Lord. 3rd Ed. 8vo. 12s.

Plumptre (Dean). — MOVEMENTS IN RELIGIOUS THOUGHT. Fcap. 8vo. 3s. 6d.

Potter (R.)—THE RELATION OF ETHICS TO RELIGION. Crown 8vo. 2s. 6d.

REASONABLE FAITH: A Short Religious Essay for the Times. By "Three Friends." Crown 8vo. 1s.

Reichel (C. P., Bishop of Meath)—
  THE LORD'S PRAYER, and other Sermons. Crown 8vo. 7s. 6d.
  CATHEDRAL AND UNIVERSITY SERMONS. Crown 8vo. 6s.

Rendall (Rev. F.)—THE THEOLOGY OF THE HEBREW CHRISTIANS. Crown 8vo. 5s.

Reynolds (H. R.)—NOTES OF THE CHRISTIAN LIFE. Crown 8vo. 7s. 6d.

Robinson (Prebendary H. G.)—MAN IN THE IMAGE OF GOD, and other Sermons. Crown 8vo. 7s. 6d.

Russell (Dean).—THE LIGHT THAT LIGHTETH EVERY MAN: Sermons. With an introduction by Dean PLUMPTRE, D.D. Crown 8vo. 6s.

Salmon (Rev. Prof. George)—
  NON-MIRACULOUS CHRISTIANITY, and other Sermons. 2nd Edition. Crown 8vo. 6s.
  GNOSTICISM AND AGNOSTICISM, and other Sermons. Crown 8vo. 7s. 6d.

SCOTCH SERMONS, 1880. By Principal CAIRD and others. 3rd Edition. 8vo. 10s. 6d.

Service (Rev. John).—SERMONS. With Portrait. Crown 8vo. 6s.

Shirley (W. N.)—ELIJAH: Four University Sermons. Fcap. 8vo. 2s. 6d.

Smith (Rev. Travers).—MAN'S KNOWLEDGE OF MAN AND OF GOD. Crown 8vo. 6s.

Smith (W. Saumarez).—THE BLOOD OF THE NEW COVENANT: A Theological Essay. Crown 8vo. 2s. 6d.

Stanley (Dean)—
  THE NATIONAL THANKSGIVING. Sermons preached in Westminster Abbey. 2nd Edition. Crown 8vo. 2s. 6d.
  ADDRESSES AND SERMONS delivered during a visit to the United States and Canada in 1878. Crown 8vo. 6s.
  THE ATHANASIAN CREED. Crown 8vo. 2s.

Stewart (Prof. Balfour) and **Tait** (Prof. P. G.)—THE UNSEEN UNIVERSE; OR, PHYSICAL SPECULATIONS ON A FUTURE STATE. 15th Edition. Crown 8vo. 6s.
  PARADOXICAL PHILOSOPHY: A Sequel to "The Unseen Universe." Crown 8vo. 7s. 6d.

Stubbs (Rev. C. W.)—FOR CHRIST AND CITY. Sermons and Addresses. Crown 8vo. 6s.

Tait (Archbishop)—
 THE PRESENT POSITION OF THE CHURCH OF ENGLAND. Being the Charge delivered at his Primary Visitation. 8vo. 3s. 6d.
 DUTIES OF THE CHURCH OF ENGLAND. . Being seven Addresses delivered at his Second Visitation. 8vo. 4s. 6d.
 THE CHURCH OF THE FUTURE. Charges delivered at his Third Quadrennial Visitation. 2nd Edition. Crown 8vo. 3s. 6d.

Taylor (Isaac).—THE RESTORATION OF BELIEF. Crown 8vo. 8s. 6d.

Temple (Frederick, Bishop of London)—
 SERMONS PREACHED IN THE CHAPEL OF RUGBY SCHOOL. 3rd and Cheaper Edition. Extra fcap. 8vo. 4s. 6d.
 SECOND SERIES. 3rd Edition. Extra fcap. 8vo. 6s.
 THIRD SERIES. 4th Edition. Extra fcap. 8vo. 6s.
 THE RELATIONS BETWEEN RELIGION AND SCIENCE. Bampton Lectures, 1884. 7th and Cheaper Ed. Cr. 8vo. 6s.

Trench (Archbishop).—HULSEAN LECTURES. 8vo. 7s. 6d.

Tulloch (Principal).—THE CHRIST OF THE GOSPELS AND THE CHRIST OF MODERN CRITICISM. Extra fcap. 8vo. 4s. 6d.

Vaughan (C. J., Dean of Llandaff)—
 MEMORIALS OF HARROW SUNDAYS. 5th Edition. Crown 8vo. 10s. 6d.
 EPIPHANY, LENT, AND EASTER. 3rd Ed. Cr. 8vo. 10s. 6d.
 HEROES OF FAITH. 2nd Edition. Crown 8vo. 6s.
 LIFE'S WORK AND GOD'S DISCIPLINE. 3rd Edition. Extra fcap. 8vo. 2s. 6d.
 THE WHOLESOME WORDS OF JESUS CHRIST. 2nd Edition. Fcap. 8vo. 3s. 6d.
 FOES OF FAITH. 2nd Edition. Fcap. 8vo. 3s. 6d.
 CHRIST SATISFYING THE INSTINCTS OF HUMANITY. 2nd Edition. Extra fcap. 8vo. 3s. 6d.
 COUNSELS FOR YOUNG STUDENTS. Fcap. 8vo. 2s. 6d.
 THE TWO GREAT TEMPTATIONS. 2nd Ed. Fcap. 8vo. 3s. 6d.
 ADDRESSES FOR YOUNG CLERGYMEN. Extra fcap. 8vo. 4s. 6d.
 "MY SON, GIVE ME THINE HEART." Extra fcap. 8vo. 5s.
 REST AWHILE. Addresses to Toilers in the Ministry. Extra fcap. 8vo. 5s.
 TEMPLE SERMONS. Crown 8vo. 10s. 6d.
 AUTHORISED OR REVISED? Sermons on some of the Texts in which the Revised Version differs from the Authorised. Crown 8vo. 7s. 6d.
 LESSONS OF THE CROSS AND PASSION. WORDS FROM THE CROSS. THE REIGN OF SIN. THE LORD'S PRAYER. Four Courses of Lent Lectures. Crown 8vo. 10s. 6d.

Vaughan (C. J., Dean of Llandaff)—*continued.*
  UNIVERSITY SERMONS. NEW AND OLD. Cr. 8vo. 10s. 6d.
  NOTES FOR LECTURES ON CONFIRMATION. Fcap. 8vo. 1s. 6d.
  THE PRAYERS OF JESUS CHRIST: a closing volume of Lent Lectures delivered in the Temple Church. Globe 8vo. 3s. 6d.
  DONCASTER SERMONS. Lessons of Life and Godliness, and Words from the Gospels. Cr. 8vo. 10s. 6d.

Vaughan (Rev. D. J.)—THE PRESENT TRIAL OF FAITH. Crown 8vo. 9s.

Vaughan (Rev. E. T.)—SOME REASONS OF OUR CHRISTIAN HOPE. Hulsean Lectures for 1875. Crown 8vo. 6s. 6d.

Vaughan (Rev. Robert).—STONES FROM THE QUARRY. Sermons. Crown 8vo. 5s.

Venn (Rev. John).—ON SOME CHARACTERISTICS OF BELIEF, SCIENTIFIC AND RELIGIOUS. 8vo. 6s. 6d.

Warington (G.)—THE WEEK OF CREATION. Cr. 8vo. 4s. 6d.

Welldon (Rev. J. E. C.)—THE SPIRITUAL LIFE, and other Sermons. Crown 8vo. 6s.

Westcott (B. F., Bishop of Durham)—
  ON THE RELIGIOUS OFFICE OF THE UNIVERSITIES. Sermons. Crown 8vo. 4s. 6d.
  GIFTS FOR MINISTRY. Addresses to Candidates for Ordination. Crown 8vo. 1s. 6d.
  THE VICTORY OF THE CROSS. Sermons preached during Holy Week, 1888, in Hereford Cathedral. Crown 8vo. 3s. 6d.
  FROM STRENGTH TO STRENGTH. Three Sermons (In Memoriam J. B. D.) Crown 8vo. 2s.
  THE REVELATION OF THE RISEN LORD. Cr. 8vo. 6s.
  THE HISTORIC FAITH. 3rd Edition. Crown 8vo. 6s.
  THE GOSPEL OF THE RESURRECTION. 6th Ed. Cr. 8vo. 6s.
  THE REVELATION OF THE FATHER. Crown 8vo. 6s.
  CHRISTUS CONSUMMATOR. 2nd Edition. Crown 8vo. 6s.
  SOME THOUGHTS FROM THE ORDINAL. Cr. 8vo. 1s. 6d.
  SOCIAL ASPECTS OF CHRISTIANITY. Crown 8vo. 6s.
  ESSAYS IN THE HISTORY OF RELIGIOUS THOUGHT IN THE WEST. Globe 8vo. 6s.
  LECTURES ON GOSPEL LIFE. Cr. 8vo. [*In the Press.*

Wickham (Rev. E. C.)—WELLINGTON COLLEGE SERMONS. Crown 8vo. 6s.

Wilkins (Prof. A. S.)—THE LIGHT OF THE WORLD: an Essay. 2nd Edition. Crown 8vo. 3s. 6d.

Wilson (J. M., Archdeacon of Manchester)—
  SERMONS PREACHED IN CLIFTON COLLEGE CHAPEL. Second Series. 1888-90. Crown 8vo. 6s.
  ESSAYS AND ADDRESSES. Crown 8vo. 4s. 6d.
  SOME CONTRIBUTIONS TO THE RELIGIOUS THOUGHT OF OUR TIME. Crown 8vo. 6s.

Printed by R. & R. CLARK, *Edinburgh*

www.ingramcontent.com/pod-product-compliance
Lightning Source LLC
Chambersburg PA
CBHW020306240426
43673CB00039B/718